SUSTAINABLE.
RESILIENT.
FREE.

SUSTAINABLE.
RESILIENT.
FREE.

The Future of Public Higher Education

JOHN WARNER

Belt Publishing

Printed in the United States of America
First edition 2020
1 2 3 4 5 6 7 8 9
ISBN: 978-1-948742-95-5

Belt Publishing
5322 Fleet Ave.
Cleveland, OH 44105

Book cover by David Wilson
Interior design by Meredith Pangrace & David Wilson

CONTENTS

PREFACE: A NEW NARRATIVE

For almost a century, the popular narrative about college in the United States has held that a college degree is the surest route to the good life. Get a college degree, and all the rest will follow. A good job, financial security, happiness, 2.2 kids, the dog, the white picket fence . . . you know the drill.

When I was growing up in the northern suburbs of Chicago in the seventies and eighties, the white child of two college-educated parents, no one had to sit me down and tell me this story. I lived it every day. Almost all the kids who graduated from the excellent public school I attended went on to four-year colleges and earned degrees. Same for their kids. Rinse and repeat, generation after generation.

I never had cause to question this narrative. For me, the story went exactly according to design. It all worked perfectly.

So, after twenty years teaching college, why am I now questioning a narrative that seems to work so well?

Well, for starters, this narrative is breaking down. Between 2013 and 2019, the percentage of American adults who agreed that college was "very important" declined from 70 percent to 51 percent. Among adults aged eighteen to twenty-nine, the population that has most recently made the choice to attend college, the decline was even sharper—from 74 percent to 41 percent.[1]

More importantly, though, for those people who aren't part of the white middle or upper class, the narrative about higher education that worked so well for my classmates and me has never really been true in the first place. White high school graduates in America are wealthier than Black and Hispanic college graduates.[2] Black and Brown students arrive at colleges and universities and often experience a steady, low-grade resistance to their ambitions that sometimes flares into outright hostility. I recall a Black student from my first-year writing course a few years ago; she had been valedictorian of her midlands South Carolina high school and she wanted to be a doctor. But she struggled on her first biology exam, an entirely common occurrence for first-year college students who are adjusting to the demands of higher education. When she sought out extra help, however, the message she received was discouraging instead of empowering. *Not everyone should major in science*, she was told. *What about social work?*

Teaching a diverse array of students over the last twenty-plus years has revealed to me how the narrative of higher education I once believed to be true—and the one I fulfilled for myself—came at the expense of people like that student.

Our most popular narratives about college haven't progressed much beyond 1978's *Animal House*, a movie that was set in 1962. *Neighbors*, the 2014 film starring Seth Rogen and Zac Efron, is practically a remake of the John Landis film. Cinematic college is so fun that even middle-aged men (*Old School*, 2003) and women (*Life of the Party*, 2018) will do whatever it takes to recreate the experience of it. College—or so the Hollywood story goes—is a place to party, a time in life where you can be casually and colossally irresponsible but still come out ok on the other side.

Times have changed.

The average GPA for the over 50,000 students who applied to medical school in 2018 was 3.57. For those who ultimately enrolled, the average was 3.72.[3] The median GPA for students who were accepted to a top ten law school was 3.865; for other ranked law schools it was 3.4.[4] When I graduated from college in 1992, with my 3.1 GPA and no particular sense of direction, I told myself that I could always go to law school if things didn't work out. And it wasn't a lie. I'm not sure what I would be thinking now.

Students today aren't having quite the same amount of fun at college either. For many of them, it is the exact opposite. According to a 2018 study by Harvard Medical School researchers,[5] one in four students had been diagnosed with a mental health disorder the prior year; one-fifth of all students had considered suicide; one-fifth reported self-injury; and 9 percent reported having attempted suicide. For many students, rather than being a happy-go-lucky interregnum before joining the "real world," as our popular and enduring fictional narratives might suggest, college is now a gauntlet to be survived.

Costs have also skyrocketed. The University of California system was tuition-free until 1968; in 1985, annual resident tuition and fees were $1,296.[6] Adjusted for inflation, that would be the equivalent of $3,105 today. Resident tuition and fees at the University of California for the 2019–2020 academic year instead totaled $14,000.[7] In 1985, it would have taken less than ten weeks of minimum wage work—not even a full summer break of labor—to fund a year's tuition and fees.[8] In 2020, even as California has the highest minimum wage of any state in the country, it would take thirty weeks.

In states with higher tuitions and lower minimum wages, things are considerably worse. At my undergraduate alma mater, the University of Illinois at Urbana-Champaign, tuition and fees range from $16,000 to nearly $22,000 a year, and the state minimum wage is $10 an hour. It could take up to a year's worth of minimum-wage work to fund one year of school. When I attended between 1988 and 1992, fifteen weeks of minimum-wage work—otherwise known as a "summer job"—would have covered the $2,200 I needed for annual tuition and fees.

According to a study by the Hope Center for College, Community, and Justice, which they conducted during the spring 2020 disruption from the coronavirus pandemic, 44 percent of two-year college students and 38 percent of four-year college students experienced food insecurity. Eleven percent of two-year students and 15 percent of four-year students lacked a stable place to live.[9] Significant numbers of students are struggling with basic necessities. How can we possibly expect them to fund tuition costs that have risen many times faster than inflation?

As the broad narrative of college being "worth it" has started to crumble, other related narratives have emerged: College is worth it if you choose the right major. College is worth it if you do the first two years at a community college. You need an education and a credential, but it doesn't have to be through college.

Each of these narratives sets aside the notion that college is the pathway to success, that it's the best time of your life, or that you can even work your way through to a degree. Rather, college is framed as an entry pass, a credential not for a prosperous and interesting life, but for an initial job after graduation. And if you don't choose wisely, you can't even expect to achieve that.

In every one of these new narratives, the benefits (or detriments) of college accrue entirely to the individual. It is a private good—even a consumer good—whose worth is literally calculated according to one's earning potential.

Colleges are about much more than this, of course. Colleges are places. They are employers and cultural hubs, institutions that serve as a locus of economic and social activity. And by allowing the narrative about higher education to become so constrained around a single goal—to get that first job—we have lost sight of this much larger role colleges play.

As I outline in the following chapters, the challenge of reorienting our public colleges and universities around a more expansive vision—one that fulfills the original mission ascribed to our public universities in things like the Morrill

Land-Grant Act of 1862—is not a problem of money and resources. The sums necessary to enact change may seem rather large initially, but relative to other, far less vital goods our taxpayer dollars go toward, they are a relative pittance. And when those costs are weighed against the massive societal benefits that may accrue from them, it will seem foolish that we haven't acted already. Rather, it is a problem of imagination. We have allowed this narrative that frames a college degree as a private good to become so enshrined that we cannot imagine it any other way. And when you throw in a global pandemic, which has upended so many of the stories we once believed to be immutably true, it's become clearer than ever that some changes, which previously seemed too radical, are just common sense.

This is, by intention, a short book. It does not include everything I would like to say. It also does not include a step-by-step plan for how we will fund public higher education with public money (though I do spend some time showing how that is very doable). The specifics and logistics of implementation will be complicated, even fraught, but before we get there, we need to better understand why tackling those details is something worth doing. This book likewise focuses only on public higher education because it is our public colleges and universities that once served as public goods but that have steadily degraded over time as they have become increasingly privatized.

If we want these institutions to survive, we don't have much choice other than to turn the page from the failures of the past and look to the possibilities of the future. If we renew these schools, the institutions where the vast majority of Americans who go to college are educated, they can play a crucial and unique role in a renewed American compact. We can write a new narrative about public higher education in America, one that actually fulfills the aspirations we claim for our colleges and universities.

PART I
DIAGNOSIS

CHAPTER 1

An Existential Crisis

The coronavirus pandemic poses an existential threat to public higher education.

And yet, I am hopeful.

While the pandemic's economic shock has exacerbated the conditions afflicting institutions of higher education, it is not the primary cause. Public postsecondary education has been ailing for a long time. And while some kind of monetary bailout will be necessary to keep colleges and universities afloat through this crisis, we also need a more significant reset that will put institutions on a sustainable path going forward.

That reset is clear. All public two- and four-year postsecondary education institutions should be tuition-free. We should also cancel all existing, federally held student loan debt. Some people might think these suggestions are far too grand. But we can achieve them if we, as a nation, can collectively rediscover our capacity for imagination.

In his recently published cultural history, *Evil Geniuses: The Unmaking of America*, Kurt Andersen argues that America has lost its hunger and ability to "improve" itself. While the quest for a more perfect union once animated American life, America since the Reagan Revolution has been significantly less innovative as a people and as a country. Innovation is something that happens *to* us, rather than *because* of us. While this has created a highly hospitable atmosphere for corporations to enrich themselves beyond imagining, it has also stifled progress and created invisible, yet very real, boundaries around our notion of what is possible.

Andersen writes, "Almost a half-century ago, the country

began a strange hiatus from its founding mission of inventing and reinventing itself in pursuit of the new and improved." He asks us to consider the upheavals the country faced in every decade of the twentieth century: the Depression, two world wars, the Cold War, the civil rights movement, the Vietnam-era peace movement, environmentalism, and others. He sees strife, of course, but also genuine progress rooted in experimentation, a willingness to not be over-beholden to the "old ways" and to move forward.

"Openness to the new was a defining American trait," Andersen observes. But this trait has largely been absent since the election of Ronald Reagan. The project of the "evil geniuses" (corporations and right-wing ideologues) in Andersen's formulation has been to realize William F. Buckley Jr.'s famous goal to "stand athwart history, yelling 'Stop!'" Or worse, to throw the country into reverse. In Andersen's view, their method for achieving this has relied on years of making our democratic republic significantly less democratic through a long campaign of gerrymandering, voter suppression, and capturing the judiciary. But perhaps more importantly, these nefarious figures have worked to shape the American psyche around what is and is not possible.

It is as though Andersen's evil geniuses convinced us that things are as good as they ever can be, and now it's just a matter of tinkering around the edges, of finding the right formula to dial in the results we desire. This illusion has been achieved by ensuring the dial has been set to a place that most advantages the corporations who fund the Republican Party and the white—primarily male—majority that supports it politically.

The innovations and societal advancements of the relatively recent past are almost inconceivable to think about proposing today. Could you imagine the government looking at a problem like poverty among the elderly and enacting a program now with the size and reach of Medicare? Today, the response to most big initiatives that could hold the potential for broad-based societal improvement and prosperity is a reflexive dismissal: *That's just not possible.*

∞

This is as true in higher education as it is anywhere else in America, but it wasn't always like this. Consider the audacity of our system of land-grant colleges, established through the Morrill Acts of 1862 and 1890. Who could imagine taking federally controlled land in every state (seventeen million acres total) and setting it aside to build institutions dedicated to agriculture, engineering, and other practical fields, while also "not excluding classical studies"? The establishment of these schools seeded our system of public universities, which have in turn benefited states in countless ways and provided economic benefits in equally countless billions and trillions of dollars. Even more recently, the 1960s saw the establishment of nearly 500 community colleges, which provided access to postsecondary education on an unprecedented scale.

For decades, up until the 1980s, America's large societal problems were identified and tackled. Possibilities were not constrained by spasms of questions concerning how we were going to pay for new programs and initiatives. The result was a century of progress. It was progress in fits and starts, and it was coupled with all of the conflict and contention that one would expect when not everyone is on board with change, but it was progress, nonetheless.

When we examine the consequences of the last forty years of public austerity and corporate largesse, however, it's clear how wrong a turn we've made. Andersen argues that now, our problems are not economic in the monetary sense—after all, prior to the pandemic, the country was richer than it ever had been—but are instead rooted in the problems of our "political economy." Big ideas and playing the long game have been subsumed by doing what it takes to win the next election cycle, or worse, the next day's news cycle. It is not a problem of money, but of vision. Andersen sees us at an "existential crossroads" in general, where we must collectively make "important choices." We are at one of those moments when it comes to postsecondary education in particular. Which path will we choose?

Collapsing Revenues

As the coronavirus pandemic rages on, the revenue sources that drive institutional operations around the country are drying up all at once. It is very, very bad. State revenues, many of which are predicated on sales and other consumption taxes, are cratering. An April 2020 projection from the Center on Budget and Policy Priorities projected an aggregated loss of $650 billion at the state level for 2020 through 2022.[1] This collapse in state revenues is happening at the same time that legislatures, on average and in aggregate, have only returned to about half of the previously reduced appropriations to higher education following the 2008 recession.[2] Charitable giving, including that to colleges and universities, will almost certainly decline in the near future. The individual incomes of students and their families will be severely affected by COVID-19, leaving them hard-pressed to fund tuition and other educational expenses. And international students, who often pay higher tuition rates at public institutions, are significantly less likely to enroll at an American university while the virus's uncertainty still looms over our ability to travel.

A huge proportion of our colleges and universities are tuition-dependent, living hand to mouth and semester to semester on the money students pay to attend. According to data from the State Higher Education Executive Officers Association, just under half of all educational revenue comes from student tuition.[3] If students fail to enroll, for whatever reason, it can mean the demise of an institution that doesn't have alternative sources of support.

It is difficult to overstate how tight margins are at most public colleges and universities. When the College of Charleston (my former employer) saw an enrollment shortfall of a total of four hundred out-of-state students over a three-year period from 2012 to 2015, the resulting $2.1 million budget shortfall resulted in "hard choices" that had the potential to "inhibit the college's ability to fulfill its mission."[4] That was a shortfall of one-half of 1 percent of a single year's total budget.

So what happens when a budget declines by 10 percent, 15 percent, 20 percent? Maybe it looks something like the University of Akron, which (as of mid-July 2020) had cut 23 percent of its full-time faculty in response to the sudden shock of the shutdowns necessitated by the pandemic.[5]

Every public college and university throughout the country is now facing similar pressures. They are shrinking their faculty and eliminating degree programs. During the 2008 recession, the institutional rhetoric often talked about "doing more with less," but even this phony optimism is absent now. In July 2020, the chairman of the University of North Carolina Board of Governors instructed the system's chancellors to prepare plans for budget cuts of between 25 and 50 percent. There is no scenario under which a university can survive after a 50 percent budget cut. That's it, game over. So long UNC-Greensboro. Been nice knowing you NC State. Godspeed, East Carolina, Appalachian State, and Elizabeth City State University. You had a nice 230-year-run, University of North Carolina-Chapel Hill, but I'm sorry to say, it's over.

And yet, even with all these horrible signs, I am hopeful.

What's beneath the Bottom?

If higher education is meant to be a ladder to prosperity, the ladder doesn't seem to reach very far and we have left out some of the rungs. Data compiled by Harvard economist Raj Chetty shows that colleges are largely stratified by socioeconomic class in terms of the students they admit. Only a few institutions in the country achieve a high "mobility rate," moving students from the bottom 40 percent of income to the top 40 percent.[6]

Much of this mobility problem is rooted in how difficult it has become to navigate college for those who do not have access to the funds to pay for it. In *Paying the Price: College Costs, Financial Aid, and the Betrayal of the American Dream,* Sara Goldrick-Rab of Temple University and the Hope Center for College, Community, and Justice shows how the byzantine system of federal and institutional aid prevents students from starting degree programs or finishing them once they've started. In one study, half of the 3,000 students Goldrick-Rab followed who enrolled in the University of Wisconsin system left college without a degree. They didn't leave because they were incapable of handling the academic demands, but because there were too many hurdles in the way of securing the basic resources necessary to live while also attending school.

To continue a program of austerity in order to keep institutions afloat through the current pandemic crisis strikes me as beyond futile. What is worth preserving about this system? And perhaps more importantly, what exactly is left to cut? Colleges and universities now are like the Black Knight in *Monty Python and the Holy Grail* who, having had multiple limbs lopped off, keeps insisting, "It's just a flesh wound!" But as Bryan Alexander, a trend tracker on higher education and the author of *Academia Next: The Futures of Higher Education,* observed in the immediate aftermath of school closures during the spring 2020 semester, "We're out of fat. We're cutting sinew, muscle, bone."

We have come to the terminus of what Christopher Newfield, a professor at UC Santa Barbara and an expert on higher education institutional finances, calls "The Great Mistake,"[7] the steady commercialization and privatization of our public colleges and universities. Having embraced the ethos of the market, we have managed to reduce the value of a postsecondary education entirely to its credential, while simultaneously leaving institutions starved of the revenue necessary to do their work.

Responding to this current crisis with the remedies of the past will consign a significant portion of institutions to a final demise. Those schools that are left behind will barely resemble what we once believed them to be, and they will turn many localities where they exist into ghost towns. Consider a school like the University of Wisconsin-Stout, which enrolls nearly 10,000 students while being situated in Menomonie, a town of 16,000 people. In many places like Menomonie, the local college or university is the town's chief employer, its cultural center, and a technology hub for the residents who surround it. To allow these institutions to die or turn into virtual shells of their former selves would be an economic disaster. Consider a Midwest that has been both ravaged by deindustrialization and stripped of its regional higher education institutions. What will be left?

If this is not enough, the total student loan debt in the United States at the time I'm writing is over $1.6 trillion. It may be noticeably larger by the time you read this sentence. The drag on prosperity that amount of debt creates is incalculable.

And yet, even with all this I am hopeful. I am hopeful because now we have little choice but to act.

CHAPTER 2

Nowhere to Go but Up

One of the reasons I am hopeful about the future of public higher education is because the threats it is facing now are not new. In fact, the reason the current crisis is so threatening is because it has been building for over thirty years. It has been a slow-motion sabotage, and the remedies are well understood.

Sadly, though, there are signs that the lessons of the past have not yet been learned. Once anyone starts asking whether or not a college education is "worth it," the inevitable end point is to reduce education to a dollars and cents return on investment (ROI), a mere credential needed for gainful employment.

The future of higher education as it is envisioned by the school of ROI is positively dystopian. Scott Galloway, an NYU marketing professor who has become a go-to voice on the future of higher education during the pandemic, sees a horizon where higher education for most people will be an almost entirely virtual experience, one where elite (primarily private) institutions will partner with giant tech companies like Microsoft, Google, and Apple to create online universities with expanded enrollments, swallowing up market share at the expense of less elite, small private schools and nonflagship public institutions.

Galloway has reduced education to its credential and decided that this is the thing of value that should be preserved; after all, the credential is what students are "buying." If an MIT or Stanford credential can be earned online at a lower cost than an in-person degree at UCLA (Galloway's alma mater), he believes it will be highly unlikely that students will choose UCLA.

Galloway recognizes this as a "reduction in humanity," but by accepting the logic of competition and credentialing, he also sees it as an inevitable development, just another business opportunity for tech companies who need to go "big-game hunting" to justify their stock prices.[1]

> Apple has to convince its stockholders that its stock price will double in five years, otherwise its stockholders will go buy Salesforce or Zoom or some other stock. Apple doesn't need to double revenue to double its stock price, but it needs to increase it by 60 or 80 percent. That means, in the next five years, Apple probably needs to increase its revenue base by $150 billion. To do this, you have to go big-game hunting. You can't feed a city raising squirrels. Those big-tech companies have to turn their eyes to new prey, the list of which gets pretty short pretty fast if you look at how big these industries need to be in that weight class. Things like automobiles. They'll be in the brains of automobiles, but they don't want to be in the business of manufacturing automobiles because it's a shitty, low-margin business. The rest of the list is government, defense, education, and health care. People ask if big tech wants to get into education and health care, and I say no, they *have* to get into education and health care. They have no choice.

This type of world isn't just in the future, either. Former Google CEO Eric Schmidt is currently working with the federal government to create something called the US Digital Service Academy, which is intended to rival Stanford and MIT in terms of funneling tech workers into government work focused on cybersecurity and artificial intelligence, exactly the type of competition Galloway envisions.[2]

Galloway sees a future where all the resources flowing toward education will be privatized. Students will be instruments to juice the stock price of our wealthiest corporations. To get an education at all will mean consigning oneself to some period of service to corporate tech overlords.

This is not me doomsaying. This plan is dictated by the logic of the market and the absolute primacy of credentialing as the purpose of postsecondary education. Galloway believes there's literally no other choice. According to his logic, colleges and universities are destined to go the way of department stores if they do not adapt to this new reality.

But what if there is an alternative?

A Fully Embodied Education

Scott Galloway has found a highly receptive audience—those keen on disruptive innovation and all that jazz—for his vision of a future where significantly expanded elite institutions dominate a primarily online space. But I am hopeful his dystopian vision will not come to pass because if our experience of the coronavirus pandemic has shown us anything, it has shown us the limits of lives lived at a distance from each other.

This is not a critique of the modality of online education. Online courses can be just as effective as face-to-face courses in terms of helping students learn. And if we are comparing a massive face-to-face lecture—like the ones I often experienced as a student at the University of Illinois—with a well-designed online course that consists of a small cohort of students and a dedicated, engaging professor, the online course is clearly superior.

But at the same time, the embodied experience of college matters. While online courses can provide excellent options for some students, they are not an adequate replacement for everybody. Those of us—like Galloway and myself—who were fortunate enough to use college not only to earn a credential but to become a more expansive person than we were before, know this to be true.

College is where I met my wife. It is where I was tested as a leader, where I both succeeded and failed as president of a fraternity. It's where I took a class with Professor Philip Graham, who counseled me toward a graduate program two years after I got my degree and then, years later, helped me secure my first college teaching job back at the University of Illinois. College is where I became so inebriated the night before an 8:00 a.m. Econ 101 exam that I vomited in the bushes outside the lecture hall and answered the multiple choice questions almost at random, receiving my well-deserved F, and where I had to ace everything else the rest of the semester to pull myself up to a B.

Animal House meets a lesson in personal responsibility.

Yes, I was credentialed with my BA in rhetoric at the end of four years, but college was also the place where I took a desktop publishing course in the early days of PageMaker and got comfortable wrestling with unfamiliar software, a skill that has paid off time and again over the course of my career. In a nonfiction writing course, we were asked to write a column that could potentially be published in a national newspaper or magazine. I chose *Esquire*,[3] and in an end-of-semester vote by my classmates, my column was voted "most entertaining." Objectively, it was probably pretty terrible, but it is impossible to quantify how much even this small encouragement meant in my overall trajectory as a writer.

I cannot imagine a life without these experiences. So why should subsequent generations be denied these opportunities simply because those who came before them lack the will to reorient the system around the values we claim are so important?

In many ways, I graduated at the last gasps of broadly affordable higher education. Just under 50 percent of the students who earned bachelor's degrees in 1993 borrowed money for their education. By 2000, that number had increased to 65 percent. In 1993, only one-quarter of those in the highest-income quartile borrowed money for college. By 2000, that number had nearly doubled.[4] That's how you end up with $1.6 trillion in student loan debt.

The system as it exists now is clearly exhausted. It seems the only place to go would look something like Galloway's vision, where tech company behemoths wield more power than the government itself,[5] and where workers will be indentured to corporations from cradle to grave. We may even be paid in digital scrip. That'll be fun.[6] Perhaps students could settle for a significantly diluted experience like a three-year degree, where the first year consists of Massive Open Online Courses (MOOCs) assessed by algorithms, a literally disembodied experience. I suppose another option would be to just give up on the notion of public higher education entirely.

But why would we go down that path if there is an alternative?

A New Narrative

I write this book as someone who deeply believes in the mission of education. I can get a little misty-eyed walking around university campuses contemplating the awesome potential embodied in such places. But I'm also someone who has been betrayed and exploited by institutions that have failed to live up to that potential.

As a career contingent (or adjunct) instructor, I have received a fraction of the pay that tenured faculty receive for the identical work of teaching credit-bearing courses. My labor has produced a surplus of tuition dollars so that others could pursue their research or teach courses that run at a deficit of tuition revenue. No doubt, I consented to these conditions with my agreement to be employed under them. But they are an injustice that is inconsistent with the academic mission. That they are entirely common to the world of higher education does not change this fact.

I know it is difficult, if not completely impossible, to divorce my view of the problems plaguing higher education from my own lived experience and frame of reference. But that's true for anyone. Galloway, the marketing professor, cannot help but see what ails institutions as a problem of branding and their need to reposition in the marketplace. My career, on the other hand, has been spent working literally below those concerns, trying to figure out how to help students learn to write. And what I've seen in this role is a system that is fundamentally hostile to that mission.

In truth, the challenges facing public higher education are not unique but are instead a by-product of the belief, which took root during the Reagan era, that markets and competition are beneficial to us all. This ethos is obviously exhausted. As we've seen, the once most-powerful country in the world has struggled to provide basic protective equipment to its frontline health care workers during a pandemic, many months after that need became readily apparent. The coronavirus is remaking society in ways we could not possibly conceive of before, revealing fault lines that many have been trying to alert us to for years and that now finally seem impossible to ignore.

I have been told by those who work in the upper levels of higher education administration that I do not understand reality, that I do not appreciate how difficult it is to meet the competing demands of student "consumers" or to manage legislatures that can be unhelpful, or even hostile, toward the aims of higher education, that everyone is doing the best they can. I do not doubt their intentions, but I question the results. If this is everyone doing the best they can, we must change course. We must make our public higher education institutions sustainable, resilient, and free.

The first step toward doing that is to understand the origins of how things went so wrong.

CHAPTER 3

The Wrong Turn

In 1983, *US News and World Report* started to rank colleges and universities. And then, over the course of thirty years or so, higher education slowly and inexorably went to shit.

We have reached the end point of what it means for colleges and universities to be run with what I call an "operations on down" approach, rather than a strategy focused from the "mission (pedagogy) on up." This is because schools are not currently in the teaching and learning business. They are machines meant to capture education-related revenue.

Carol Christ, the current chancellor of the University of California, Berkeley, made it plain in a 2016 interview, "Colleges and universities are fundamentally in the business of enrolling students for tuition dollars."[1] In other words, as explicitly stated by the leader of one of the top public universities in the country, in our system as it is currently structured, colleges and universities are not oriented around the mission of teaching and learning, but instead exist to recruit students, enroll students, collect tuition, and hold class—operations. Oh, also football.[2]

These conditions are not unique to public higher education. We are experiencing the final reckoning of the failed promise of Reagan's America in almost every sector of society, where deregulation and the resulting competition was supposedly going to unleash the unstoppable force of the free market to deliver superior and cheaper goods and services for everybody.

In 2020, however, there's been no shortage of stark evidence of the sheer exhaustion of governance rooted in Reagan-era faiths like minimal government, minimal regulation, maximum competition, and a privileging of profits over sustainability and broad-based prosperity. The lurching governmental response to the coronavirus pandemic, wherein states have been largely left to their own devices as they attempt to "reopen" in order to spur economic activity, despite the obvious consequences of increased infections, is an object example. People are literally being asked to sacrifice their lives for the good of the stock market.

There is little thirst or imagination for structures which privilege safety or prudence over the profits that are accruing to a narrow group of corporations and individuals. The turmoil surrounding campuses' attempts to reopen for face-to-face instruction in the midst of an unchecked pandemic speaks to the dysfunction and sickness of the present system. Colleges have to open because they must collect fees for room and board. They're bringing students into coronavirus hot zones and making those zones even hotter, or they're creating new hot spots in places where conditions were previously promising—all in order to protect the bottom line.

As we compare life in America to other wealthy countries similarly affected by the virus, we can see how misguided the vision of Reagan's America truly has been.

The Great Unravelling

Other public goods besides higher education have been terribly degraded over the last four decades as well. Competition in the newspaper industry has left us with three national behemoths (the *New York Times*, the *Wall Street Journal*, and the *Washington Post*) while hundreds of regional papers are barely hanging on. Formerly great newspapers like the *Denver Post* and *Chicago Tribune* have been drained by the private equity firm Alden Global Capital, using various (and legal) financial shenanigans to drive up debt and extract profits before leaving the discarded husk behind.[3]

The decline in local journalism is an object lesson in how the loss of a public good can come at significant cost to the public. In the long run, it is the municipalities who are deprived of a robust fourth estate watchdog that suffer when local newspapers shutter. A comprehensive 2018 overview by the *Columbia Journalism Review*[4] found that in the absence of local reporters to hold them accountable, local governments are less responsive, less engaged, and more corrupt.

A similar phenomenon is now playing out in health care. After the emergence of the coronavirus, the elective procedures that drive profits in the industry are being canceled, leading to layoffs and furloughs of medical personnel in the middle of a pandemic.[5] Health care organizations—even nominally not-for-profit ones—are oriented around revenue collection as opposed to actual public health outcomes. Just like the world of local journalism, the Rube Goldberg nature of our overarching health care system has left an opening for private equity to drive up costs as they extract profits[6] while degrading both the quality of care and the job satisfaction of health care workers. Not coincidentally, the cost of health care at the state level has led to a decrease in funding of higher education institutions;[7] colleges and universities are also finding their operating budgets getting eaten up more and more by skyrocketing health care costs.

In 1983, the Reagan administration published *A Nation at Risk*, which warned the country about "a rising tide of mediocrity" in the nation's K–12 schools. The report, authored by the US National Commission on Excellence in Education, kicked off almost forty years of educational reforms—most clearly embodied by President George W. Bush's No Child Left Behind and President Barack Obama's Race to the Top initiatives—which have been predicated on the idea of competition, primarily around raising standardized test scores.

It's become apparent, however, that the tests students

were asked to prepare for have been unworthy of their time. Results have remained stagnant, and students are experiencing ever-increasing levels of anxiety, depression, and suicide. Even reformers are now admitting that maybe they got some things wrong.[8] Meanwhile, educational corporations like Pearson, which peddle both the standardized tests and the materials to prepare for them, have profited to the tune of billions of taxpayer dollars.

The truth is that competition is a lousy framework for education. Requiring students to compete with each other for increasingly narrow pathways to success has indeed left lots of children behind. Even the winners are stressed out and demoralized, alienated from the pleasures of learning. By privileging operations, we've lost sight of education's true mission. That's just as true at colleges and universities as it is at K–12 schools. We should see the Reagan-era faiths and narratives for what they are—false and bankrupt programs that are literally bankrupting us.

CHAPTER 4

Competition Is Bad for Public Higher Education

With rankings comes competition, and in the current systems of higher education rankings, the only avenues by which colleges and universities can compete are prestige and amenities. Neither of those categories has anything to do with the underlying quality of education students get at the institution itself.

Believe it or not, the original incarnation of the *US News* Best College Ranking, which was released semiannually from 1983 to 1987, relied entirely on a peer reputation survey. Imagine a situation where your rating of a restaurant was based solely on what you had heard from others, rather than from any kind of firsthand experience. This is the exact kind of methodology that kicked off our college ranking obsession. Over the years, *US News* has tweaked its formula so that the peer reputation survey only accounts for 20 percent of the current rankings' overall total, but the criteria they've added—graduation rates (35 percent); faculty resources (20 percent); financial resources (10 percent); student excellence, meaning high school class rank and test scores (10 percent); and alumni giving (5 percent)—overwhelmingly favor wealthy institutions that serve wealthy students. In 2020, nineteen of the top twenty institutions were private; UCLA came in at number twenty.

Prestige became a proxy for quality when in reality, it was just a marker for wealth.

But the narrative about the importance of prestige took hold inside institutions as well. Prestige could draw new students, which in turn could drive a school's tuition revenue.

And for the vast majority of public institutions, as state support has melted away year after year, that revenue has become the primary source of funding.

In 1960, 78 percent of the University of Michigan's general fund budget came from the state, and just over 20 percent came from student tuition. Now, more than 75 percent of the budget comes from student tuition; 14 percent comes from the state.[1] Because of these shifts, tuition increases have been outpacing inflation since the 1980s. But they were particularly pronounced in the aftermath of the 2008 Great Recession. Tuition in Louisiana, Arizona, Hawaii, and Georgia increased by over 75 percent between 2008 and 2017 as a direct result of declining state contributions. Forty-one states saw an increase in tuition of more than 20 percent over this same period.[2] By the end of 2019, tuition accounted for 46 percent of all education revenue.[3] This will almost certainly get worse during and after the pandemic.

Asking institutions that are financially strapped to compete as though they are wealthy requires them to burnish a "brand." But when that brand isn't supported by actual substance, we run into real problems.

Sending a Brand to Do an Institution's Job

Donald Trump is what happens when you send a brand to do an institution's job. His incompetent performance as president during a major national health crisis has validated the fact that he not only is not up to the job, but that he also has no interest in it. Rather than digging in to do the job of the president of the United States, he has instead spent the entirety of his presidency fluffing the Trump brand.

Now, when a college or university becomes a "brand," it is not de facto a bad thing. When brands reflect an authentic underlying reality, when being good at the thing your organization does is good for the brand, brand and organization are a virtuous partnership. If it really was true, as Trump claimed about himself during the 2016 campaign, that "I alone can fix it," and he actually did fix things, he would have become quite popular.

In the era before the *US News* rankings, colleges and universities were not so much brands as they were "types." The elite were the elite. Flagship state universities were generally interchangeable. Regional publics were all "good schools." There may have been slight differences in selectivity or the test scores of incoming students for similar types of institutions across states, but these reflected regional differences, not some inherent special quality of the institution itself.

But the *US News* rankings provided a blueprint by which institutions of the same type could improve their brand relative to the other schools in their close cohort. Institutions could also strive to move up in terms of their class. Unfortunately, the disconnect between the rankings' criteria and what is actually good for the quality of education created a classic case of what is known as Goodhart's law: "When a measure becomes a target, it ceases to become a good measure." Because the *US News* rankings are almost exclusively a measure of inputs, rather than outputs, influencing the rankings merely requires schools to figure out how to admit the kind of students who will bolster their ratings.

I saw this process take shape firsthand during my years as a non-tenure-track lecturer at Clemson University between 2005 and 2011. Upon assuming the Clemson presidency in 2001, James F. Barker declared a goal of moving the university from thirty-eighth place into the top twenty of *US News*'s public university rankings, a rather bold pronouncement given the low probability that other institutions would falter themselves. Clemson would have to leap over them. And as Catherine Watt, an institutional researcher at the university during this era, recounted, Clemson's quest largely involved finding more and more creative ways to juke the stats.[4]

In order to boost faculty salaries, Clemson increased student tuition and started including the cost of benefits to the data they reported to *US News*. The school rejiggered accounting practices in order to report the most favorable financial information to the ranking board, even though that information was all on paper and ultimately meaningless to the university's on-the-ground operations.

Since class sizes below twenty were a key element in the rankings, Clemson lowered the enrollments of as many twenty- and twenty-five-person classes as it could. But it simultaneously increased the enrollments of classes with fifty-five students to seventy. Most infamously, in order to give Clemson's relative rating a boost, Watt reported that school officials participating in the reputational survey rated every other program in the entire country "below average."[5] She also remarked that she believed other schools were doing this as well, quoting a colleague who said, "People don't have this as their official vision, but by God, it's their unofficial vision." Some other schools dispensed with the machinations altogether and simply lied. For example, between 2005 and 2011, Claremont McKenna College submitted false SAT scores in order to boost its ranking.[6]

During this time, I recall an official from Clemson's provost's office inviting all non-tenure-track lecturers to a meeting, a rare occasion indeed. In the English department at the time, non-tenure-track faculty taught more than 70 percent of the total course offerings; each of us made $25,000 a year for teaching four courses per semester. Some of the lucky ones (including me) were eligible for health insurance. Others were not. The provost office official had a proposal: because the percentage of faculty with terminal degrees mattered in the rankings, wouldn't it be a great idea if those of us without terminal degrees pursued a PhD in our spare time?

We had questions. Would Clemson help fund these pursuits? No. Would there be new titles or raises if we completed these programs? No. So why would we want to spend our time doing this? For the rankings!

Clemson ultimately did reach its goal. The school hit number twenty in 2015 before falling back to number twenty-three the following year. Currently, they're at number twenty-nine. Admittedly, the school's machinations did result in some improved metrics. Freshman retention increased from 82 to 89 percent, and the graduation rate rose from 72 to 78 percent. But unfortunately, those improvements came coupled with a move away from the mission of providing access to educational opportunities for the citizens of South Carolina. This pattern has played out at public universities and colleges across the country.

Country Club Public Universities

A 2018 report[7] from New America, a nonpartisan—though more like a center-with-an-essence-of-left-leaning—think tank, illustrates how the chase for prestige in a privatized higher education marketplace has closed off educational opportunities for low-income students. Authored by New America analyst Stephen Burd, the report shows how the percentage of schools with an average net price—the cost to students after grant and scholarship aid is deducted from tuition and fees—above $10,000 increased from 34 percent in 2010 to 52 percent in 2015. As Burd notes:

> Over the last 20 years, state disinvestment and institutional status-seeking have worked together, hand in hand, to encourage public colleges and universities to adopt the enrollment management tactics of their private college counterparts. For many of these schools, that has meant using their

institutional aid dollars strategically in order to lure affluent out-of-state students to their campuses, rather than spend these funds on in-state students who can't afford to go to college without help.

In other words, the chase for prestige has subsumed higher education's mission of access and opportunity. Merit aid is used as a tool to enroll "desirable" students while aid for low-income families languishes.

Burd identifies a class of what he calls "country-club public universities," schools that have a low net price but that also admit low numbers of students who are eligible for Pell Grants, a trait that is consistent with using merit aid to enroll desirable students who help in the rankings. Schools with a net price under $10,000 that also enrolled fewer that 15 percent Pell-eligible students include some of the highest ranked public universities in the country: the University of Virginia, the University of Michigan, the University of Wisconsin-Madison, and the College of William and Mary. These are public colleges where large proportions of the student body are carved out for rich people. At William and Mary, for example, 56 percent of students come from the top 10 percent in terms of household income. Only 2 percent come from the bottom 20 percent.

Burd notes how a commitment to maintaining need-based aid actually hurts institutions in the competitive landscape. The University of Illinois, which still gives the bulk of its aid based on need, has made itself vulnerable to other states' poaching of Illinois residents. According to Burd, "These carpetbagger recruiters have been remarkably successful. Today, nearly half of all Illinois students leave the state to go to college. That's up from less than one-third back in 2000."

Schools who chase prestige but lack the resources of schools like William and Mary or the University of Virginia are not "country-club universities." They're just plain expensive. This problem is particularly acute in states where legislatures have largely abandoned support for public institutions. The effect on Pennsylvania schools is particularly striking in this regard. Temple, the University of Pittsburgh, and all of the Penn State campuses have net prices over $16,000 per year. Historically Black colleges and universities (HBCUs), which enroll large proportions of Pell-eligible students but couple that with high net prices, also fall into this category. South Carolina State has a 67 percent Pell-eligible student body with a net price of over $21,000. Grambling enrolls 82 percent Pell-eligible students at a net price of almost $17,000. This category also includes the University of Alabama, the University of Colorado-Boulder, the University of Kansas, and, you guessed it, Clemson University.

All of this leads to a system where highly similar public schools attempt to poach students from each other's states in order to be able to realize the increased revenue available through nonresident tuition. Applicants from Virginia who are rejected by Virginia Tech will instead enroll at Clemson, and applicants from South Carolina who are rejected from Clemson will instead enroll at Virginia Tech. This inevitably drives up costs for all students.

The situation has gotten so dire that it has become a trend for wealthy parents in the Chicago suburbs to sever their guardianship of their children so those children will be eligible for Pell Grants and other need-based aid.[8] This was attempted by one family with a household income over $250,000 a year; they were living in a $1.2 million dollar home, but their savings had been tapped out by spending $600,000 on their children's educations. Yes, we can judge these people for making the choice to send their kids to expensive colleges and living above their means, but they too are products of a dysfunctional system. But in the end, thanks to those who figure out how to game the system whenever it even slightly disadvantages them, it is the low-income students who are harmed the most.

Please pardon my language, but if our public colleges and universities are supposed to serve as an ecosystem that provides access to economic opportunity regardless of the accident of your birth, this is some fucked-up shit. We have broken faith with millennials and the members of Generation Z. The promise that hard work will translate into opportunities for education and prosperity is gone. And it isn't the pandemic that killed it.

To break this cycle, we must recognize that we cannot view education as a consumer good any longer. Education—public education—is infrastructure, and we should treat it that way.

CHAPTER 5

Public Education
Is Infrastructure

Call me a soft-hearted dreamer, but I believe postsecondary education should aim to develop the intellectual, social, and economic potential of students while also engaging with the needs of the broader local, state, and national communities in which its institutions operate. Public colleges and universities should serve as engines of prosperity beyond the monetary fortunes of individual students, even as they take great care to provide opportunities for all students.

It follows then that public education is infrastructure. It belongs in the same category as our roads, bridges, utilities, municipal services, parks, libraries, and everything else we need for society to operate as a collective.

When infrastructure breaks down or doesn't exist, we see outsized hardship. Nationwide, broad swaths of the population have lived this truth in the struggle over how to reopen K–12 schools during the pandemic; in the absence of school, we can see how difficult it is for parents to work and for children to socialize and develop. And if we desire a prosperous, well-functioning society that offers everyone a reasonable chance at moving up the ladder of prosperity, postsecondary education is no less vital than K–12 education is. But to understand postsecondary education as infrastructure, we must take a more expansive view of what college means and what parts of it are meaningful.

While there is significant fervor around so-called STEM jobs and other high-demand industries, research cosponsored by Gallup and Purdue University reveals that a happy life after college is not tied to where you get your degree or what your field of study is; instead, it's tied to what you experience when you are in school. The survey measured people's "engagement" with their work, as well as their overall "well-being." Unsurprisingly, being engaged at one's work makes someone four times more likely to be "thriving" in terms of overall well-being.[1]

The survey found that being engaged at work was at least twice as likely if respondents agreed with any of the following statements concerning what they experienced while in college:

- I had a mentor who encouraged me to pursue my goals and dreams.

- My professors at college cared about me as a person.

- I had at least one professor who made me excited about learning.

Unfortunately, only 14 percent of the postgraduates surveyed could say they agreed with all three of these statements. But these are precisely the experiences colleges should be focusing on.

Structuring education as an enterprise in which institutions compete with each other for the same supply of students, and in which students compete with each other for the vanishing number of paths to economic security, has resulted in a dysfunctional ecosystem overall. Competition is not entirely foreign to ecosystems, but in a healthy ecosystem, one needn't become a top predator or risk extinction. The shark needs those little fish that clean its teeth, just as the little fish that clean the shark's teeth need the shark. A sustainable ecosystem houses a community of interconnected elements that all interact with each other in a way that ideally allows every participant to thrive in its particular role. Unfortunately, in order to be successful—or more accurately, just to survive—we've tasked our public colleges and universities with becoming great white sharks, or at least crafting a reasonable appearance to make them look like one. I hope I've made it clear how exhausted this model has already become.

Fortunately, the pieces for a truly cooperative ecosystem are already in place in the world of higher education. Our system of two-year colleges, regional publics, and statewide flagships could quite easily be repurposed around a common mission of fitting students with opportunities while also allowing much easier movement among these different layers by crafting no-questions-asked credit transfer agreements among them.

This requires thinking about public higher education as an entire interdependent ecosystem rather than a series of individual institutions. We want each individual institution to be excellent, but we also want each school to be excellent in the specific role they play and the particular niche they fill. Part of this involves making sure that public money goes to the public mission, which means we have to talk about the role of private institutions in a public ecosystem.

The Role of Elite Private Colleges and Universities

Reading the title of this book, someone might reasonably ask, "What do you have against *private* colleges and universities?" The answer is . . . nothing. They are part of the overall ecosystem of higher education and they should be considered as we shape a future where public money is used to fund the public good of a postsecondary educational infrastructure.

But we should also clearly understand the current position of private institutions within the ecosystem of higher education, particularly in terms of how few people they educate relative to the whole and how significantly a small proportion of elite private schools currently benefit from public funds.

This is particularly true of our most well-heeled private institutions. They may dominate the public discourse around education, but they make up a very small part of the whole. For example, the undergraduate enrollment for the entire Ivy League is roughly equivalent to that of Ohio State. The undergraduate enrollment for the New England Small College Athletic Conference (NESCAC), which includes elite small liberal arts colleges such as Amherst, Williams, and Middlebury, is one-half the size of Michigan State.

As a whole, nonprofit private colleges and universities enroll approximately 17 percent of the students who are pursuing postsecondary education in a given year in the United States. That's larger than a rounding error, but it remains a decidedly minority share. If we are seeking to create a system of higher education that is open and accessible to as many qualified students as possible, private colleges and universities, particularly of the elite variety, just do not matter.

Another reason why elite private institutions are irrelevant in terms of reshaping the higher education ecosystem as an engine for broad-based prosperity is that these schools overwhelmingly serve students who are already prosperous. The Raj Chetty data on economic mobility reveals that the median annual family income for students at Ivy League institutions is between $150,000 and $200,000. Two-thirds of their students come from the top 20 percent in terms of income. While graduates of Ivy League colleges who started in the bottom 20 percent income bracket have a better than even chance of moving up to the top 20 percent bracket, fewer than 4 percent of Ivy League students come from the bottom 20 percent to begin with.

This means that fewer than 900 individuals per year are put on track to move from the bottom to the top of the income ladder by graduating from an Ivy League institution.

As a vehicle for increasing prosperity, the Ivy League is the equivalent of a go-cart or worse, a riding lawn mower.

We spend a disproportionate amount of energy trying to create a level playing field for students to compete for slots at elite schools, but highly selective institutions—those schools that accept fewer than 25 percent of applicants—make up only 4 percent of all colleges and universities. This outsized emphasis on elite institutions distorts where attention and resources actually flow in the overall education ecosystem.

In contrast, 80 percent of four-year schools accept more than 50 percent of applicants. If we add in two-year, open-admission colleges, we can see how limited the benefits of trying to boost less advantaged students in the competitive race for admissions are going to be when we consider postsecondary education as a cooperative ecosystem that maximizes overall prosperity. Much of this mania around boosting precollege achievement and "leveling the playing field" simply has no chance of creating a positive effect for large numbers of students.

Consider how one of our most prominent educational philanthropies, the Chan Zuckerberg Initiative (CZI), which has provided over $100 million for education grants since 2018, directs its money and influence. The CZI mission statement declares:

> Every child should enter adulthood with the knowledge, skills, habits, and agency they need to realize their full potential. We believe that applying what we know from the fields of learning science and human development to education is the most promising way to achieve this vision.[2]

One CZI program, "Vision to Learn," seeks to fulfill this mission by making sure all children have basic eye care. This is laudatory. By definition and design, it expands access to education and educational resources. But other CZI programs, such as customized SAT practice through Khan Academy, a nonprofit educational organization that provides online tutorials, show the limits of an ecosystem that asks students to compete for scarce slots at selective institutions rather than maximizing their opportunities to benefit from attending *any* institution. Success on the SAT is not correlated with success in college. Nor is it truly reflective of aptitude, as the testing companies claim. Instead, average SAT scores are correlated with household income. Improving on the SAT is not a useful thing for its own sake. Ultimately, charitable efforts at leveling the playing field by helping students strive to attend a selective institution do little to help those students who will attend nonselective institutions, *which is the vast majority of them!*

I sometimes think our perceptions have been so warped by the ethos of competition that we cannot see a way toward genuine equity and opportunity. For a time, so-called "undermatching"—the fact that qualified students from minority backgrounds and low-income families are less likely to pursue admission at selective institutions of any kind— became a focus of researchers' attention. College leaders across the country pledged to address this problem.

It didn't work. The percentage of students who were deemed "undermatching" didn't budge. Even with some aid, selective private colleges remained unaffordable for the vast majority of students. Meanwhile, public institutions like CUNY, which serve so many, are being decimated by budget shortfalls.[3]

The real barrier is not that students need more information about elite schools or special encouragement to apply. The far bigger problem is that undermatched students are simply more likely to lack the economic resources necessary to complete a degree at *any* college or university.

And it gets worse. Undergraduate admissions to elite

institutions are also rigged.

I am not talking about the infamous admissions scandal that snared Aunt Becky and her fashion designer husband along with other well-heeled folks. I'm not even referring to the entirely aboveboard legal bribery that was a $2.5 million pledge to Harvard by real estate developer Charles Kushner in advance of the matriculation of his son Jared.

Rather, I am talking about a status quo that is designed around perpetuating generational privilege. At Harvard, for example, 43 percent of admitted white students between 2009 and 2014 were legacies, athletes, children of donors, or children of faculty. Athletes and legacies have admission rates of 87 percent and 34 percent respectively, while the rate for general admits is less than 5 percent. Admitted students who are legacies, children of donors, or children of faculty are five times more likely to be white than Black. Athletes are twice as likely to be white than Black.[4] At elite liberal arts colleges such as Amherst and Williams, that compete in Division III of the NCAA, 79 percent of the student-athletes are white. They compete in sports such as crew, lacrosse, sailing, and field hockey, which predominate in wealthy East Coast communities.[5] Division III schools cannot offer athletic scholarships, but 75 percent of these athletes receive some form of merit or need-based aid.[6]

If the Chan Zuckerberg Initiative wants to help students from low-income, predominantly minority families gain admission to elite private colleges and universities, it may be more effective to offer them access to sailing or fencing lessons rather than SAT prep.

The snarky take on this phenomenon is that colleges and universities are practicing "affirmative action for rich white kids." But this is a mischaracterization. Affirmative action, in its original conception, was intended to address historic, systemic inequities of opportunity. Subsequent court rulings have instead allowed affirmative action only in the interests of enhancing "student diversity," but the underlying problem of unequal access remains largely unaddressed. Admitting rich white kids is the system working as designed.

These inequities are not only apparent in elite private institutions; they have trickled down to selective public colleges and universities as well. A 2020 report from the Education Trust, titled "Segregation Forever?" finds that the 101 most selective public colleges and universities enroll a smaller percentage of Black students today than they did twenty years ago. While the total number of Hispanic students has increased, the increase is smaller than the growth of the Hispanic population overall.[7]

The title of the Education Trust report invokes the words of George Wallace's 1963 inaugural speech as governor of Alabama, when he declared his resistance to the civil rights movement by declaring "segregation now, segregation tomorrow, segregation forever." We are almost sixty years removed from Wallace, decades into what colleges and universities would claim are good faith attempts to provide equal access to Black students. It has not worked.

The problems are clearly structural, and as selective public schools have tried to emulate elite private institutions, it has resulted in a dysfunctional, inhospitable ecosystem.

Most Open, Most Equitable, Least Resourced

If we consider our postsecondary educational institutions as an ecosystem, we can easily see one sector that receives considerably less sustenance than the others: community colleges. Private four-year colleges spend, on average, $72,000 per full-time student each year. At four-year public institutions, it's $40,000 per student. At community colleges, that figure is $14,000 per student.

Community colleges are frequently criticized for having low graduation rates, but judging these institutions on this criterion is nonsensical. A student who transfers early from a community college, where they're pursuing an associate's degree, to a four-year institution is a good thing, not a strike against the community college. An adult learner coming back for a couple of courses to bolster their skills is a vital part of a community college's role in the community it serves, and yet this may ultimately count against the college itself when it comes time to assess its "effectiveness."

Because money tends to follow prestige, open-access institutions consistently get short shrift in terms of per-student funding. But rather than investing time and money into helping a small proportion of those students from lower-income households compete for a limited number of slots at elite private institutions, what if we instead *funded* the schools where students from the lowest-income quintile already attend? And what if we found some of the money necessary to do this from the disproportionate amount of tax breaks and public subsidies accrued by our wealthiest private colleges and universities?

Livin' Large on the Public Dime

Much is made of the massive endowments of schools like Harvard ($39 billion), Yale ($30 billion), Stanford ($27 billion), and Princeton ($26 billion), but these are not the only sources of wealth that elevate these institutions above the average public college or university.

In 2015, Nexus Research sought to quantify the "hidden public cost of private non-profit colleges." As nonprofit entities, these institutions are exempt from local, state, and federal taxes. They do not pay property taxes, nor are they taxed on investment income generated by their endowments.[8] These clear public subsidies, "hidden" from scrutiny, are often not considered when accounting for the public money that's spent on our larger higher education ecosystem. But this current situation clearly shows that our wealthiest private universities receive massive public subsidies on a per student basis.

For 2013, the year studied by Nexus, Stanford University's nonprofit status meant it benefited from an annual $63,100 subsidy per full-time student. At California's flagship university, Cal Berkeley, the annual subsidy was $10,500 per student. In Connecticut, Yale receives $69,000 per student while UConn receives $23,300. In Illinois, the University of Chicago receives $19,300 per student while the University of Illinois receives just $7,500. New Jersey has perhaps the most egregious gap between the haves, the have-somes, and the have-nots. Princeton's yearly subsidy per student comes in at $105,000. Rutgers's is $12,300. At Essex Community College, that figure is $2,400. The list goes on and on.

The traditional argument for these tax breaks and subsidies is that private colleges and universities are engaged in a mission directly related to the public good. And undoubtedly, there are private colleges that take this mission seriously. For example, out of 614 selective private colleges, Trinity College in Washington, DC—alma mater of Nancy Pelosi, among others—ranks 590th in terms of median parental income ($37,600 per year). The average student there comes from the forty-first percentile for income. By comparison, students at Duke come from families in the eight-second income percentile on average. But Trinity, with its explicit mission to enroll low-income students, is the exception.

The wealth disparity between our richest private colleges and universities and all the others is akin to the wealth disparity between our richest billionaires and the rest of the American populace. Jeff Bezos, Warren Buffett, and Bill Gates collectively have more wealth than 160 million Americans combined.

It's time to spread that wealth.

CHAPTER 6

What about the University
of Everywhere?

I n part two of this book, I'm going to present my vision for a sustainable, free, resilient public institution of higher learning, and it will be glorious. Or at least plausible. But first, we must consider an alternative model—the "University of Everywhere."

The University of Everywhere is a specific coinage taken from the 2015 book, *The End of College: Creating the Future of Learning and the University of Everywhere*, by Kevin Carey, who directs the education policy program at New America. I'm using Carey's book as a primary example here, but in the aftermath of the 2008 recession, as states reneged on their responsibility to fund postsecondary education, and as tuition subsequently continued to climb, the notion that it might be possible to deliver a postsecondary credential that was both cheaper than and superior to a traditional two-year or four-year degree took root among a broad swath of education reporters, consultants, and wonks. In addition to Carey's book, for example, there was NPR education reporter Anya Kamenetz's *DIY U: Edupunks, Edupreneurs, and the Coming Transformation of Higher Education,* Ryan Craig's *College Disrupted: The Great Unbundling of Higher Education*, and Jeffrey Selingo's *College Unbound: The Future of Higher Education and What It Means for Students.*

It is important to note that all these books were written in good faith by people who are deeply invested in supporting the cause of education and the interests of students. Kamenetz is one of the top education journalists in the country. Selingo has advised college presidents. Craig is an educational entrepreneur and venture investor; though he has a worldview about education that I personally often find troubling, if he's acting entirely out of greed, education is the wrong place to ply his trade. Carey's career has been dedicated to various causes of education reform as well. (You'll notice that I have used New America's research approvingly elsewhere.) I imagine each of these writers would say they want to reform and improve the system of higher education for the benefit of students.

While there was some variation among these different books, their general thrust was the same. College was expensive, they argued, and student money was paying for frivolous amenities, which was driving up the cost of tuition and fees. Students also weren't learning much. But thanks to new developments in technology, it could all be done much better. And much more cheaply.

This narrative spread beyond reporters and wonks. In one week in June 2015, both Chris Christie and Elizabeth Warren criticized colleges and universities for overspending on amenities. Christie lamented schools were "drunk on cash and embarking on crazy spending binges." In a speech to the American Federation of Teachers, Warren remarked, "Some colleges have doubled down in a competition for students that involves fancy dorms, high-end student centers, climbing walls and lazy rivers—paying for those amenities with still higher tuition and fees."[1]

When prominent political figures from both parties are sharing the same narrative, you know it has significant traction, even though the idea that public colleges and universities are "drunk on cash" is absurd.

Here's the thing, though, the "university of everywhere" narrative—college is expensive, amenities are an important cause of increased tuition, students aren't learning, and technology can help do things better and more cheaply—just simply wasn't true.

The Non-Scourge of Lazy Rivers

Yes, some colleges and universities have lazy rivers. No, they are nowhere near ubiquitous. As with many narratives peddling the tale of colleges gone wrong, the same handful of cases are cited in article after article and left to stand in for what is, in reality, an incredibly diverse array of institutions.

One of the institutions that's most frequently tagged with this charge of frivolous lazy river-ism is Louisiana State University, which, at the time of Christie and Warren's criticism, was spending $85 million to refurbish its recreation facilities, even as its tuition was rapidly increasing. But the actual story is more complicated. LSU's existing infrastructure, like many schools that were founded hundreds of years ago, was in bad shape and needed replacement. Unlike lots of campus building construction, which tends to get financed through bonds that subsequent generations of students pay for in increased tuition without having any say in the matter, LSU's recreational complex was approved through a direct vote of students who overwhelmingly agreed—84 percent to 16 percent—to an increased recreation fee to cover the cost of renovation.

Undoubtedly, we can question LSU's decision to focus on upgrading amenities before addressing the school's academic needs, but this was a textbook case of a university acting according to the logic of the marketplace in which it was tasked to compete. *Schools are in the fundamental business of enrolling students for tuition dollars.* Amenities are just one of the available avenues for competition. The fault is in the structure of a system that makes it necessary for schools to install these kinds of luxury amenities in order to stay solvent in the first place.

And even if we ultimately want to find fault with LSU or the University of Alabama or Texas Tech for spending on fancy water features that they believe will attract students, there are more than 1,600 nonprofit public colleges and universities in the United States. Perhaps two percent of them (or even fewer) have these kinds of amenities. And honestly, if you've experienced southern Louisiana's weather between the months of March and October, you too might relish access to a lazy river.[2]

If you want a more accurate picture of the construction that truly drives up the cost of student tuition, check out the bond debt that public institutions must assume because state legislatures have refused to appropriate funds to replace decaying physical infrastructure. For example, close to my home, South Carolina's public postsecondary institutions collectively owe $2.7 billion in principal and interest payments that are to be paid through 2047. Because the money for these payments comes from tuition revenue, full-time students take on more debt, and annual tuition costs increase.[3] At South Carolina State University, student debt averages $26,335 per student, and tuition has increased by $984 per year. At Clemson, debt is $26,309 per student and tuition has increased by $1,414 per year. And at USC Columbia (including the School of Medicine and four other smaller campuses), debt averages $14,623 per student and there's been a $920 increase in tuition per year.

When you walk around these public campuses, you will definitely see a few new, splashy buildings, but those may be replacing literal crumbling wrecks. Other spaces may be severely neglected. My office at the College of Charleston, in an undoubtedly charming building dating from the mid-1800s, had a mold problem so severe that I could not be inside with the windows closed for more than an hour without risking an attack.

Before we condemn the choices of these institutions, consider the game of competition they've been asked to play without being given the resources necessary to compete.

"Students Aren't Learning"

The narrative that college students aren't learning anything and that we should therefore embrace the "university of everywhere" is largely traceable to a single book—*Academically Adrift: Limited Learning on College Campuses* by sociologists Richard Arum and Josipa Roksa. Jeffrey Selingo's invocation of this study in a June 2017 article for the *Washington Post* is pretty typical of how Arum and Roksa's book has been used as evidence that students aren't actually learning anything in college.[4]

> A seminal study in 2011 that resulted in the book *Academically Adrift* found that one-third of college students made no gains in their writing, complex reasoning, or critical-thinking skills after four years of college. "American higher education is characterized by limited or no learning for a large proportion of students," wrote authors Richard Arum and Josipa Roksa. For many undergraduates, they wrote, "drifting through college without a clear sense of purpose is readily apparent."

This single study became a kind of gospel among those who were seeking to reform higher education. It was utilized as a cudgel to either browbeat institutions into changing their ways or to induce accreditors to look at other educational providers as legitimate alternatives.

But the narrative of students not learning much of anything begins to crumble when we realize this single study made use of a single standardized test, the Collegiate Learning Assessment (CLA), to draw its most major conclusions. The CLA (now the CLA+) is no worse—and its somewhat better—than the average standardized test, but it is still a standardized test, which comes with all the instrument's limitations. For example, it utilizes a "performance task," where one interacts with a number of "documents" in order to develop analytical responses to specific questions. It is an example of what I call "snow globe" critical thinking, where the test creates a world that resembles ours, but that must be hermetically sealed off from it lest the testing instrument be tainted by prior or outside knowledge.

A performance task like this can test a way of thinking, but it is not a test of knowledge. It certainly isn't a test of what someone has learned. To truly be able to think critically means being able to compare some new bit of information to an existing body of knowledge. Critical thinking also involves one's personal frame of reference and value system. To set these aside in a test of critical thinking is not to test critical thinking at all, and the fact that this test has been used to demonstrate that students aren't learning is simply dishonest.

If performance on the CLA+ is evidence that college is broken, the most broken school in the country is state flagship the University of Texas at Austin, where seniors scored below the freshmen. The City College of New York, which has the second-highest income mobility rate in the country, also has a negative value-added score on the CLA+. So does Ohio State.

Critiques of both the methodology and findings of *Academically Adrift* are numerous, as they should be![5] Subsequent research using the same data as Arum and Roksa, but using different methodology for analysis, found that students had in fact made gains in critical thinking as measured by the CLA.[6]

Is the CLA actually a good measurement tool to find out whether or not students are learning anything in college? Or should we instead look to a tool like the Gallup-Purdue Index, which measures "experiences" that correlate to postgraduate engagement in work and happiness in life? Surely this too is a type of learning.

Kevin Carey used *Academically Adrift* to declare the claims of college being "worth it" as "bankrupt."[7] He did this because, in 2015, he thought we were going to be saved by the University of Everywhere. But where is it now, when we seem to need it more than ever?

A False Hope
In *The End of College*, Kevin Carey describes "the University of Everywhere":

> The University of Everywhere will span the earth. The students will come from towns, cities, and countries in all cultures and societies, members of a growing global middle class who will transform the experience of higher education.

These students will be educated in digital learning environments of unprecedented sophistication. The University of Everywhere will solve the basic problem that has bedeviled universities since they were first invented over a millennium ago: how to provide a personalized, individual education to large numbers of people at a reasonable price.[7]

Carey paints a vision of a personalized education, "driven by advances in artificial intelligence and fueled by massive amounts of data," where "information about student learning will be used to continually adapt and improve people's educational experience based on their unique strengths, needs, flaws, and aspirations." He portrays legacy institutions as "decadent," places where venture capitalists and entrepreneurs can arrive to save the day. Why not enable students to take courses from the best faculty in the world, for only the price of an internet connection?

Even better, in the mind of Anant Agarwal, founder and CEO of the MOOC provider EdX (a joint venture of Harvard and MIT), would be a lesson delivered by Matt Damon. "From what I hear, really good actors can actually teach really well," Agarwal said in 2013. "So just imagine, maybe we get Matt Damon to teach Thévenin's theorem," he added, referring to a concept that Agarwal covers in a MOOC he teaches on circuits and electronics. "I think students would enjoy that more than taking it from Agarwal."[8] I suppose the only question is if Damon would deliver the material as himself, or if he would slip back into character as the troubled math genius Will Hunting.

Here's what I have to say about all that: wishing does not make it so. Teaching is not synonymous with information delivery.

In reality, Carey's vision of the university of everywhere was dead before his book even arrived. MOOCs, in which a student is fed a canned curriculum asynchronously alongside tens of thousands of other students, turned out to be the opposite of a personalized education. A pilot program for a course using Udacity's MOOC for math credits at San Jose State University was ended early because students in the traditional courses taught by San Jose State faculty were doing significantly better.[9] MOOC completion rates overall were 5 percent or less. In 2013, Udacity cofounder Sebastian Thrun declared his own company's MOOCs "a lousy product."[10] Thrun has since moved on from Udacity, now serving as president and CEO of Kitty Hawk Corporation, a manufacturer of battery-powered personal air vehicles, a demonstration of the kind of dedication to education that is common among those who are most certain that they can disrupt it.

The Myth of Personalized Learning

The idea that algorithms can figure out what students need to learn and then place the best possible lesson in front of them on a just-in-time basis is an attractive notion to some, but in truth, it's not rooted in any sort of observable reality.

It is vaporware, nonexistent software. It can assume the shape of anything the purveyor can dream up, which perhaps explains why it remains so attractive as a method of improving education. But we must not buy into this myth.

Larry Berger, one of the founding figures in personalized learning software through his startup, Amplify, admitted to prominent right-wing education reformer Rick Hess in 2018 that his idea of a map that could chart what students know and what they haven't learned yet, and where software could figure out the best place to put students on the map at any given time, was a fantasy.

For years, Berger believed, "If the map, the assessments, and the library were used by millions of kids, then the algorithms would get smarter and smarter, and make better, more personalized choices about which things to put in front of which kids."[11] But there was a big problem. As Berger put it himself, "The map doesn't exist, the measurement is impossible, and we have, collectively, built only 5 percent of the library." Even more importantly, "Just because the algorithms want a kid to learn the next thing doesn't mean that a real kid actually wants to learn that thing." Carey, and other educational reformers who spin a tale of technology riding to the rescue, had a compelling narrative that played into our particular American biases of a belief in innovation and progress, of the power of the free market to improve our lives.

Audrey Watters, a historian of educational technology, and sociologist Sara Goldrick-Rab, both with a subject matter expertise superior to Carey's, wrote a critical response to *The End of College* in the immediate wake of its publication, highlighting some of the problems I discuss here along with many more.[12] They note something important about the narratives we attach to higher education, namely who gets to tell them, and who is listened to:

> In this political economy, the experts on education
> are rarely experts in education, and that is just the
> way an increasing number of powerful people seem
> to like it. Books like these and the speeches and
> essays accompanying them eat up the landscape
> of popular discourse. With the microphone, these
> voices have the gravitas of maleness and whiteness
> and wealth. They are so loud they *must* be expert.
> They look like, walk like and talk like leaders.

Kevin Carey is a frequent contributor to the *New York Times* and heads education policy at one of America's most prominent think tanks. Jeffrey Selingo, a former editor at the *Chronicle of Higher Education*, can be read in the *Washington Post*, and he directly advises Michael Crow, president of Arizona State University. These men wield tremendous influence over education policy without being experts *in* education. They are not educators.

As we look to create sustainable and resilient public universities, one of the things we must pay attention to is who we pay attention to when we're thinking through our greatest challenges. It is not that we must shut out voices like Carey and Selingo, but their contributions must be contextualized and complemented by others with an actual expertise *in* education.

Carey's vision of the University of Everywhere was obsolete before it was published, and yet his story of decadent institutions that needed disrupting joined a chorus of others singing a similar tune, eroding belief in the idea that our public colleges and universities are indeed part of our larger public infrastructure, and thus deserving of our support. It did a lot of damage that will be difficult to undo. Fortunately, faced with the crisis of the coronavirus pandemic, people now seem to be rallying around the needs of public colleges and universities.

And one of those people is Kevin Carey.

They Paved Paradise and Put Up a Parking Lot

If there has ever been a historical moment ripe for the University of Everywhere to step into the breach, it is the crisis of the coronavirus pandemic. As institutions struggled with the spring transition to emergency distance learning, and as uncertainty loomed over plans for the fall, however, there has been no stampede of students toward alternative online providers.

In fact, it has been the opposite, with school officials often insisting that face-to-face schooling is an absolute necessity. In a *New York Times* editorial on May 5, 2020, Carey, who five years previously was describing higher education as a failed enterprise, sounded the alarm over the coming budget crisis for public colleges, declaring, "the public in public college could be endangered."[13]

If the past predicts the present, Carey wrote:

> public college and university budgets will be slashed, sending tuition and student loan debt skyward. Some institutions will be so starved of funding that they will effectively cease to be 'public' at all. Others will have a greatly diminished ability to help students learn. . . . Cutting universities loose to compete for customers in the free market could fundamentally alter the character of public institutions.

So what gives?

Part of it is that we've come to realize that there is little desire among students for the alternatives provided by the University of Everywhere. MOOCs have a niche to fill, but they are not a sufficient substitute for a course taught by an experienced instructor to an appropriately sized cohort of students. Even as many instructors have been laboring in less than ideal, and even hostile conditions, students recognize the value in a fully embodied education. And of course, the enforced physical separation of the pandemic has revealed the less quantifiable pleasures and benefits of in-person social interaction.

The full narrative about college—that it is a place where students can develop their intellectual, social, and economic potential at an institution that is engaged with the needs of the broader local, state, and national community—appears to be a resilient one. Now it's just a matter of working to make sure this story becomes a reality.

PART II
THE CURE

CHAPTER 7

The Possibilities of Tuition-Free Public Higher Education

All public two-year and four-year postsecondary education institutions in the United States should be tuition-free. America should also cancel all existing federally held student loan debt.

This is the cure for higher education's current ailments.

Tuition-free public higher education is necessary because it is the only way to reorient colleges and universities around the mission of teaching and learning. As long as schools are in the fundamental business of enrolling students for tuition dollars, we will continue to see all of the problems outlined in the first part of this book. There is no hope of reforming a system that is fundamentally misaligned with our desired objectives.

There is no more powerful illustration for this need than the "clusterfuck"[1] of attempts by various large public institutions to open up for residential living and face-to-face instruction in the middle of a global pandemic. Colleges have lured students back to campus with guarantees and contingency plans for managing COVID-19, but when the fall semester began with nearly instant outbreaks, colleges have blamed students for engaging in behaviors that were entirely foreseeable. It all perfectly illustrates the desperation at work. Any plan that relied on near-universal compliance with rules around social distancing and social gatherings was doomed to fail—not because college students are different from any other group of people but because they are the same.

If colleges and universities were not tuition-dependent, they could have assessed the difficulties posed by the start of the fall 2020 semester from a fundamentally different perspective. Rather than treating students as customers just long enough to get them to commit to the semester—and then suddenly treating them not only as stakeholders, but as *saviors* of the institution, requiring a kind of monastic discipline from them—schools could have planned with the greater good in mind.

Consider the public missive from J. Michael Haynie, a vice chancellor at Syracuse, after a hundred or so students gathered on the university's quad prior to the start of classes. He accused the students of "selfish and reckless behavior" before explicitly threatening them:

> All this said, I want you to understand right now and very clearly that we have one shot to make this happen. The world is watching, and they expect you to fail. Prove them wrong. Be better. Be adults. Think of someone other than yourself. And also, do not test the resolve of this university to take swift action to prioritize the health and well-being of our campus and Central New York community.

Here we see an institution that had done everything possible to convince students that they should return to campus for the fall and then pivoted seamlessly to criminalizing typical student behavior.

If colleges and universities were not tuition-dependent, they could have also used the summer months to plan for an online semester instead of making an ill-fated attempt at face-to-face instruction that has now resulted in a greater disruption to learning and subsequently sent scores of students from their COVID-19 hotspot campuses back to their home communities.

Many institutions will argue they had no choice but to

make these attempts, that to declare an intention to stay online would have resulted in a loss of students to other institutions that were determined to provide a residential experience. I personally believe this concern was overblown. Schools that made an early declaration to go online have not been unduly harmed when it comes to enrollment, and it appears that many students and their families have appreciated the transparency and clarity.[2]

But I am also sympathetic to the catch-22 many schools must have believed themselves to be facing. As I write, mere weeks into the fall 2020 semester, the results have been terrible. Schools like the University of North Carolina at Chapel Hill, Purdue, NC State, Syracuse, and others are at open war with segments of their own student bodies. The reputational damage and fracturing of relations among stakeholders will be lasting. Observing the carnage, Tressie McMillan Cottom, a professor at UNC-Chapel Hill, declared, "I truly believe that the way universities are breaking their covenant with students during this pandemic will not be forgotten for a generation. What a way to blow a couple hundred years of trust."[3]

Removing the financial necessities that are driving these difficulties would allow public higher education to return to its position of what it once was and should be—a public good. By making institutions truly resilient and responsive to public needs, they will become sustainable. The public need in this current moment is to do the best we can to keep college students moving forward in their educations without exacerbating the spread of a deadly pandemic. Unfortunately, because of the structures underlying public higher education, colleges and universities had no chance of accomplishing that public good. In fact, it barely even came up.

Tuition-free colleges and universities aren't some kind of outrageous fantasy. In fact, they were once rather common. The University of Florida didn't charge tuition until 1969.[4]

The City University of New York (CUNY) system didn't start charging tuition until 1976.[5] The University of California system was chartered in 1868 with an explicit promise to be free to California residents. It was California Governor Ronald Reagan who first proposed that institutions start charging tuition;[6] at first, Cal Berkeley President Clark Kerr resisted the move, but by 1968, the school had instituted a $300 "registration fee." By 2012, student tuition at Berkeley accounted for $3 billion in revenue, while state appropriations were $2.3 billion.

Tuition-free systems are not entirely a thing of the past either. The Tennessee Promise program has made all two-year colleges in the state tuition-free, a program which has increased enrollment, degree attainment, and students' rate of transfer to four-year institutions.[7] Colleges and universities are now more complicated and expensive entities to run than they were in the late 1960s,[8] but the idea that tuition costs should not be a barrier to college is hardly a novel idea. Even for schools that were not tuition-free, low, accessible tuition rates were common into the 1980s. Much of the Rube Goldberg apparatus of our federal financial aid system is predicated on fulfilling the mission of making college "affordable" to anyone who qualifies.

So if we already agree on the underlying goal of affordability, and if it's already been done before, why not take the most efficient road to that goal while also achieving the maximal version of it now?

How much is this going to cost? As David Deming, director of the Malcolm Wiener Center for Social Policy at the Harvard Kennedy School, wrote in the *New York Times*, "not as much as you'd think."[9] Using data from 2019, eliminating tuition at all public colleges and universities would cost around $79 billion a year. To put that figure in context, in 2016, per the most recent data available, the federal government spent

$91 billion "on policies that subsidized college attendance."[10] There we go. It's done, and with $12 billion left over.

The reality is somewhat more complicated, of course, but it is important to note that the federal government already invests enough in its attempt to make higher education affordable that we could make public institutions tuition-free.

Different plans have different figures, which is to be expected for something so complex. Bernie Sanders's plan would add $47 billion a year in federal funding on top of what states and the federal government already spend. Simply fixing federal payments at current revenue levels would only serve to reinforce existing inequities, so we should add additional money into the ecosystem through state-federal partnerships. We should also seek to support private institutions that have proven records of admitting students from lower rungs of the socioeconomic ladder, as their missions are also broadly aligned with the public good. Killing off private institutions that meet our collective goals is in no one's interest. But when it comes to the wealthy elites, it's time to end the subsidized gravy train they've been riding for decades.

Given that it will take several more decades for public institutions to catch up to what those elite private institutions have realized in terms of public subsidies, consider this a balancing of the scales. Remember also that public institutions annually enroll more than 80 percent of all students in college nationwide.

While the need to shift to a tuition-free public system is straightforward and, to my mind, obvious, the implementation of a plan like this will be complex, requiring a gathering of stakeholders in pursuit of this shared goal. Those complexities will have to be solved, just as NASA had to figure out how to get to the moon, and states had to build their universities in the first place following the granting of land under the Morrill Acts. But the first step is to believe that this is not only worth doing, but that it is absolutely necessary.

We must remember what it is to believe in progress.

Making Amends

In addition to making public colleges and universities tuition-free, we must also forgive all existing federally held student loan debt. Debt forgiveness in some form was a central feature of just about every 2020 Democratic presidential candidate's platform, and while any steps we take toward achieving this goal would be an improvement over the status quo, the maximal approach of total forgiveness is most desirable for several reasons.

First, it is the easiest and most straightforward plan to implement. All student loan debt held by the federal government can be forgiven with the flip of a switch. Any plan with cutoffs for income or loan amount runs the risk of being buried in red tape and in the end will be much less efficient and efficacious. There is a long history that says universal benefits are more popular than means-tested programs. Let's get it right the first time.

Second, similar to making the choice to embrace the goal of tuition-free public postsecondary education, doing something big and bold will restore public faith in the government to act in ways that benefit the citizens they serve. As Chris Newfield argued at the *Chronicle of Higher Education*, "Only a much bigger vision of what college is really for will inspire the expanded public investment that the system desperately needs. And everyone who wants to see higher education flourish should be going to the mat to make this vision possible and popular."[11]

Finally, the macroeconomic benefit of this kind of stimulus will be significant during a recession, particularly when there is bipartisan agreement that economic stimulus is necessary. A 2018 analysis by a group of economists at the

Levy Economics Institute at Bard College explains how and why canceling student loan debt provides so much bang for the buck.[12] Using the total of $1.4 trillion in student debt at the time of the analysis, the authors calculated that there would be $100 billion in GDP growth per year over a ten-year period if debt were forgiven. Unemployment would be reduced by between one-quarter and one-third of a percent.[13] Inflationary effects were almost nonexistent, as were the effects on state and federal budget deficits. As a source of comparison, the signature Trump tax cut cost $1.5 trillion and has had a far greater impact on the national debt; the money has gone to wealthy people who are less likely to put it back into circulation. In contrast, the majority of student loan debt is held by regular folks. Though canceling the debt will mean the government will collect less revenue, those figures will be offset by increased economic activity.

What kind of increased activity? For one thing, people would have more children. A 2018 *New York Times* poll asked people between twenty and forty-five why they might be having fewer kids than desired, or why they had fewer kids than they had planned. Economic concerns—the high cost of childcare, overall worry about the economy and personal financial stability—were the most cited reasons.[14] Removing this albatross from the necks of so many young people could also spur additional small business activities and entrepreneurship. It would be a crucial financial cushion as we navigate the recessionary downturn of the COVID-19 era.

There would even be benefits for those of us who do not hold any debt. Without the load of student debt, millennials and members of Generation Z might be better able to afford my house when it is time for me to cash in my biggest asset and ride into the retirement sunset. Shared prosperity makes for a more dynamic economy and greater investment in public goods. Our atrophied spirits will be revived by this demonstration that it is once again possible to do big things and to take real steps toward progress.

Perhaps more important than all of this, however, is the fact that forgiving student loan debt is simply the right thing to do. We have broken faith with younger generations when it comes to providing access to the American dream of life, liberty, and the pursuit of happiness. The risk of taking on student loans was supposed to pay off with greater earnings, which would allow students to swiftly repay them. But as economist Marshall Steinbaum observes, "Instead, the labor market credentialized, reducing the earnings associated with any given level of attainment. So people needed to take on more debt to get more degrees just to get the same jobs earning the same wages."[15] There was no pot of gold at the end of the rainbow. There wasn't even a pot of silver or bronze. Once solid, middle-class professions like teaching—which require college degrees, and often even advanced degrees—have been turned into quasi-priesthoods with concomitant vows of poverty.

Undoubtedly, some people will see larger benefits from debt cancellation than others. But all of us will share at least a little bit in the prosperity. And once we prove that we know how to act in the name of progress, we may just be able to do it again and again.

CHAPTER 8

Mission over Operations

In the first part of this book, I explained the fundamental disconnect between the demands of a capitalist market economy and the needs of a broad-based ecosystem of postsecondary education. For a public good like education, competition is the route to inequality, not excellence; it leads to waste, not efficiency. But even though upending this system by making it tuition-free will go a long way toward putting colleges and universities on a sustainable and resilient path, it is not a sufficient solution by itself.

The narrative of public higher education's dissolution has its villains. Misapplied market economics, shortsighted politicians, heartless administrators, and faculty who turned a blind eye to the erosion of shared governance as long as their personal privileges were maintained have all played a role in the process. But while there have been some genuinely malevolent actors—particularly in the political ranks—and while there are others who have allowed visions of grandeur to lead them to shortsighted acts with negative long-term consequences, in my view, the vast majority of people who are involved in the operations of higher education believe strongly in the mission of public colleges and universities.

And yet, those same people who have dedicated their lives to these institutions have been presiding over them as they've descended inexorably and steadily downhill over a period of decades. All that splashy marketing copy meant to impress prospective students and goose one's *US News and World Report* ranking is a gloss over the underlying widespread erosion of the mission of teaching and learning.

So how can people who truly love and value something also be complicit in its collapse?

I can start trying to answer this question by asking it to myself. I have spent many hours wondering why I worked for so long as a college instructor for so little pay—never more than $36,000 per year as a full-time employee—carrying student loads that reached as high as triple the recommended disciplinary maximum for the teaching of writing. Writing about libraries and librarians, Fobazi Ettarh coined the term "vocational awe," "the set of ideas, values, and assumptions librarians have about themselves and the profession that result in notions that libraries as institutions are inherently good, sacred notions, and therefore beyond critique." Ettarh believes that it is precisely this vocational awe which makes librarians accept low salaries and that makes them so vulnerable to burnout.[1] To the person operating with a sense of vocational awe, the institution is so important that self-immiseration is a worthwhile tradeoff.

That's me, only with teaching instead of librarianship.

During the semester, I didn't dwell on the conditions under which I worked—that not only included low pay, but also overcrowded offices, some of them with actual health hazards—partly because I was too busy to dwell on them. But I also didn't want to kill the part of me that was clearly being nourished by teaching. It was easy to convince myself that what I was doing *mattered* because the evidence was right in front of me. There are few professional pleasures equivalent to seeing a student switch from the off position and into the on position when it comes to their writing. And even when conditions were at their worst, I would experience a flush of importance as I fancied myself a bulwark against the system's degradations. I wasn't just important, I told myself, I was *necessary*. Without me, where would the students and the school be?

The pleasures of martyrdom only carry so far, however,

and I only lasted as long as I did because I was materially secure due to my secondary income from writing and editing and my marriage to a well-employed partner. But even this security allowed me to convince myself that of course I had to stick with teaching; unlike others, I could *afford* to be paid so little.

My willingness to grind myself to the nub each semester in order to deliver a meaningful educational experience, despite working under conditions that were highly hostile to that goal, ultimately made me complicit with the perpetuation of this terrible system. It's fucked up, honestly. I feel like an idiot even admitting to this mentality, but it illustrates how belief can paper over structural and systemic problems.

I am hardly an outlier in my experience. Adjunct and contingent faculty now comprise the majority of instructional faculty in higher education. The system has been able to sustain itself thus far because there is a ready supply of individuals who are willing to throw themselves into the breach, either because of a love for the work and a belief in the mission or because they still hold out hope of becoming one of the tenured elect.

Institutional Awe
I do not think that "vocational awe" explains the actions of college administrators, particularly high-level ones, but perhaps there is a related condition—"institutional awe."

Colleges and universities are amazing places. Quite a few that are still around today predate the existence of the United States. The physical grounds of many of our large state universities are a marvel. While urban commuter schools may not have the same architectural grandeur as a sprawling land-grant university complex, to walk into a campus building in the midst of a busy city is to feel the energy of thousands of people simultaneously pursuing something meaningful. It is hard to be inside a college or university and not feel its deep *importance*, to convince yourself that it is the institution itself that matters above all else.

I do not know how else to explain the fact that administrators from the University of North Carolina at Chapel Hill, for example, chose to open their campus to face-to-face instruction in the midst of an unchecked global pandemic, despite their state's own health officials recommending against it and having insufficient contingent plans to manage an outbreak.[2] It's possible UNC's chancellor, Kevin M. Guskiewicz, believed the mitigation measures the university had undertaken were sufficient to keep students safe. Reporting by Jeremy Bauer-Wolf at *Education Dive* also suggests that the ultimate decision to open the UNC system's campuses rested with the board of governors, "a historically dysfunctional panel beset by partisanship" that had been kept on a "tight leash" by the "Republican-dominated legislature."[3]

Guskiewicz may have felt, and even been genuinely powerless to resist, the board's edicts, but his public statements suggest a commitment to reopening even in the face of pleas from university faculty, staff, and students to either delay the start of in-person instruction or to move the entire fall semester online in the interests of safety. His university was sued in a class action by campus workers.[4] Student groups hosted die-ins, and each announcement of new cases on campus prompted additional cries of concern. UNC's community was undeniably, and possibly permanently, fractured from these events. And for what? After one week of classes, COVID-19 infections overwhelmed the campus and UNC switched to total remote instruction.

The only way to arrive at this state of affairs is to believe that the institution itself is *more important* than the people and the community that institution serves. If some number of faculty or staff or students must get sick or develop a chronic disability or even die to preserve the institution, then that is what must be done.

I do not mean to impugn Guskiewicz specifically. He was in an incredibly difficult position. He has spent the vast majority of his career at UNC and he must love the place. I am certain he was motivated by what he felt was best for UNC writ large, and when you have a state governing board above you that is calling for up to a 50 percent budget cut, the threat must appear truly existential. At least he and other campus leaders were transparent in sharing data and in their decision to pivot back to remote instruction before more damage was done. This sadly is not true for all colleges and universities in the United States.

But if an institution going about its business is actively harming those it is meant to serve, we are in a state of deep dysfunction. We need to stop being awed by the operation of colleges and universities and instead focus on the actual work those institutions do, the work of teaching and learning. As UNC puts it in its own mission statement, "Our mission is to serve as a center for research, scholarship, and creativity and to teach a diverse community of undergraduate, graduate, and professional students to become the next generation of leaders."

While making public colleges and universities open and accessible to all who qualify requires us to embrace a tuition-free model, that solution itself isn't enough to cure all the ills plaguing American higher education. Institutions that are designed to survive in our dysfunctional system will also need to fundamentally reconceptualize some of the core practices that have been churning forward for decades. For example, schools that have been attempting to survive by competing for nonresident students and their greater tuition dollars will no longer need three dozen out-of-state recruiters when 90 percent of its students are from in-state. The seven-figure salaries of university presidents who are viewed as fundraising Jedis or as politician-whisperers to particularly intransigent or hostile legislatures will not only be unnecessary, they'll be impossible due to the constraints imposed as a condition of the federal aid necessary to make institutions tuition-free. Reforming governing boards so they're something other than political fiefdoms is also necessary, and perhaps could also be a contingency tied to increased federal funding.[5]

This remaking will require some root-level discussions about what truly matters. Deciding what matters will require identifying and then living by the values that are consistent with the sustainable, resilient, and free university. Let's start right now with the lives and work of faculty.

PART III
RECOVERY

CHAPTER 9

Teaching and Learning:
The Core of the Sustainable,
Resilient, and Free Public
Institution

The core of the sustainable and resilient college or university is the mission of teaching and learning. Tuition, after all, is meant to cover the cost of instruction. If public money is going to substitute for student tuition, it follows that it should go toward funding the instructional mission of a college or university.

Presently, particularly at research universities, it does not. In fact, student tuition subsidizes all manner of what is commonly called "departmental research." This is probably going to have to stop. It is going to have to stop because the mechanism by which this research work has been protected is through the steady "adjunctification" of faculty, a process that has only worsened over time. It's at the point now where three-quarters of all faculty are non-tenure-track.[1]

I spent the entirety of my teaching career as a nontenured lecturer or adjunct instructor. When I was in a "full-time" position, I taught a minimum of twelve credit hours per semester. My colleagues who were tenured or on the tenure track at the three Research I institutions where I worked[2] were tasked with teaching six credit hours.[3] Tenured faculty were also required to produce "research" while I was only responsible for teaching my courses, but they also routinely made three times my salary. I also published extensively during this period, but I was not compensated for this work as part of my employment. This situation was most stark at Clemson, where I taught four courses per semester and was paid $25,000 per year; tenured faculty there made *at least* $75,000 per year.[4]

My nontenurable colleagues and I were literal human shields protecting the privilege of tenured faculty to do their research, which was largely funded by student tuition. This practice of tuition subsidizing noninstructional labor by tenured faculty is so ubiquitous that up until now, it has been beyond question. But it's incompatible with a publicly funded, sustainable institution.

Though it is quite difficult to come up with a firm calculation of how the cross-subsidies inside a college or university work, Charles Schwartz, emeritus professor of physics at the University of California, Berkeley, calculated that 40 percent of undergraduate tuition at his own institution went to subsidizing faculty research.[5] His calculations suggest a massive subsidy direct from students to faculty work that has, at best, a tangential relationship to students' experiences at the institution. There may be some justification for a portion of tuition supporting faculty research that impacts the quality of instruction, but it is not justifiable for 40 percent of tuition dollars to go toward that purpose.

Faculty Are Laborers, Not Knowledge Workers

Tenured faculty sometimes like to think of themselves as "knowledge workers"—people who are paid to think for a living, and whose thoughts have value in the world. I am a fan of knowledge work. I spend a fair amount of time doing it myself. Knowledge work needs no economic justification to be worth doing. Thinking for a living generates things that previously didn't exist, which is awesome and necessary. And in an ideal world, research and teaching are part of a virtuous circle, each feeding the other.

But it is dangerous for faculty to look only at the *kind* of work they do and declare themselves to be knowledge workers, because in our capitalist system, most faculty research, particularly in the humanities, has very little tangible economic value. Knowledge workers like engineers or architects produce things (i.e., building plans) that others will pay for. This is not true for most faculty, however. Most academic research is part of a "gift economy"—in which something is given without an explicit agreement for immediate or future rewards—rather than a free market capitalist one.[6] While academic publishers make money from faculty research (by selling it back to libraries; what a deal!) they rely on the institutions themselves to make the economics of the gift economy work by bestowing increased compensation and security upon tenured or tenure-track faculty.

It is regrettable but true that most of this research has almost no economic value in a capitalist system. This reality has been dawning on state legislatures who somewhere between suspicious of and hostile to what they believe is going on at their public institutions. Faculty are being required to "justify" their work, which means a cold calculation around cost and value.

Knowledge work is important, and a return to public funding may revivify broader public belief in the value of research, but how can we claim it as a vital part of the work of college faculty when an ever-shrinking minority of faculty are actually able to pursue this kind of work as part of their compensated job duties?

At their core, all faculty are laborers. That labor is supported by student tuition. The functioning of the institution must support this reality.

In their role as human shields, nontenured faculty are paid less for the identical labor of teaching. This is the very definition of an unsustainable practice, and it is demonstrably damaging to a university's institutional mission. Having a majority of precariously employed instructors—who are often scrambling to make ends meet by cobbling together work at multiple institutions or by working second jobs—do the bulk of the instructional work is not in anyone's interests, and yet it is the status quo.

There has been much lip service and hand-wringing over this state of affairs, but very little action. No one likes it, but we are apparently powerless to do anything about it. But when our institutions are funded by public money rather than by student-provided tuition, this situation can be remedied. It's pretty straightforward.

Teaching Labor Equity Wage

My contention is simple. Identical work should earn an identical wage. The way we measure the amount of work for teaching in higher education is the credit hour. This also happens to be how we calculate how much students pay in tuition, so we should use the credit hour as the basis for comparing work across different categories of academic laborers.

Our ultimate goal is to determine the Teaching Labor Equity Wage and then make sure all laborers earn that. But to do this, we must first calculate the Teaching Labor Wage Gap, which requires aggregating the salaries of all faculty who teach at least one class, determine what portion of those salaries is dedicated to instruction, and then do a little addition, multiplication, and division.

For simplicity's sake, let's imagine an academic department that's equal parts tenured faculty making $88,000 per year, assistant professors making $67,000 per year, lecturers making $35,000 per year, and adjuncts who teach two courses per year and who make $3,250 per course.[7]

Calculation of Dollars Earmarked for Teaching	
Tenured Professor	$88,000 salary, 2/2 load (4/year), 40 percent teaching, 40 percent research, 20 percent service. Teaching labor salary: $88,000 x 0.4 = $35,200. Per course wage: $35,200/4 = $8,700.
Assistant Professor	$67,000 salary, 2/2 load (4/year), 40 percent teaching, 40 percent research, 20 percent service. Teaching labor salary: $26,800. Per course wage: $6,700.
Lecturer	$35,000 salary, 4/4 load (8/year), 100 percent teaching. Teaching labor salary: $35,000. Per course wage: $4,375.
Adjunct Professor	$6,500 salary, (2/year), 100 percent teaching. Teaching labor salary: $6,500. Per course wage: $3,250.

The total amount earmarked for instruction is $103,500, and with eighteen total courses taught, the average per course wage across all ranks is $5,750. This means the equity wage gap would come to:

Tenured Professor: $8,700 - $5,750 = $3,050
Assistant Professor: $6,700 - $5,750 = $950
Lecturer: $4,375 - $5,750 = -$1,375
Adjunct Professor: $3,250 - $5,750 = -$2,500

The lower pay of nontenure faculty is directly subsidizing the higher pay of tenure and tenure-track faculty for the *identical labor*. Remember that I'm only counting the portion of tenured job descriptions that are dedicated to teaching.

Redistributing the pool of money ostensibly earmarked for instruction on an equitable per course basis ($5,750/course) would change the salaries by rank like this:

Tenured Professor: $75,800 (previously $88,000)
Assistant Professor: $63,200 (previously $67,000)
Lecturer: $46,000 (previously $35,000)
Adjunct Professor: $11,500 (previously $6,500)

Questions and Answers

When I provide this information to faculty, particularly tenured faculty, I am often confronted with what I think of as "but what about?" questions, which are, in my mind, attempts to rationalize existing inequities. I deal with these contentions in the following ways:

QUESTION: I know that the description of my job says that I only spend 20 percent of my time on service, but it's way more than that in terms of hours worked, so your calculation doesn't reflect the reality of my work. What do we do about this?

ANSWER: There are several responses to this. The first is one of sympathy. As the proportion of tenured faculty has shrunk, the tenured faculty who remain must do more service. While adjunct faculty are more heavily disadvantaged by this system overall, tenured faculty are disadvantaged as well. But we can only go by the stated definition of the job for our calculations. If faculty jobs are truly 50 percent service, this is primarily an indication of how out of whack the balance of labor has become due to adjunctification. This is a problem with the labor structure of higher education, not the calculation itself. We should similarly acknowledge that adjuncts also do a significant amount of uncompensated work around service, including developing curriculum, writing recommendations, and even doing peer reviews if they are still striving for a job on the tenure track.

QUESTION: What about big-time-endowed-professor types, who are hired as much for their eminence as they are for their teaching? How do we handle them?

ANSWER: Simply adjust the portion of their labor that reflects their teaching. If they're doing one course a year, they're obviously getting paid for their reputation, not their instruction. Say that 10 percent of their job is teaching. This calculation seeks only to make the labor of teaching equitably paid work. Everything else is untouched. You'll find that the superstar faculty are likely extremely well paid for the teaching portion of their labor, even when they teach very few courses.

QUESTION: Shouldn't tenured faculty, having been at a school longer and having established seniority, deserve a higher per course wage?

ANSWER: Adding a multiplier for seniority and length of service in the department is perfectly defensible, but for equity's sake, it must be applied regardless of rank. For example, contingent faculty with twenty years' service should receive the same multiplier as a full professor who has been at a school for the same duration of employment.

QUESTION: Upper-division courses that tenured faculty primarily teach require more expertise. Shouldn't that be rewarded with a greater per course wage?

ANSWER: Here we get into a discussion of labor and values. I would argue that the expertise is already baked into the proportion of the tenured faculty's salary dedicated to research. We also are opening a whole can of worms about what we mean in terms of "expertise" when it comes to the labor of teaching. Rank is not an indicator of teaching expertise, and there are many adjunct faculty who could quite capably teach upper-division courses if given the opportunity.

If we believe that these upper-division courses require more *labor*, one could argue for more per course, but is this true? I've taught up and down the curricular ladder, including graduate classes, and in general, the time spent on the labor *decreases* as one moves up. The most "difficult" course I have taught in terms of the amount of labor it requires is first-year composition.

Still, it's a discussion worth having. Just make sure that the grounding is in equity—equal wage for equal work—rather than in seeking to find a rationale to justify higher pay (for teaching alone) for higher rank. Prestige is not labor.

QUESTION: How do you think this would look at different kinds of institutions?

ANSWER: It would be interesting to see. I'm confident that the teaching wage equity gap is largest at public research universities, where tenure and tenure-track faculty typically teach two courses per semester, and that it would shrink as you move down the Carnegie classifications, where tenured faculty teach more while also being required to do service and research. It's possible there are some places where tenured faculty have been squeezed so hard that the teaching labor equity wage gap is much smaller or nonexistent. There is often a large teaching labor equity wage gap at community colleges that rely on lots of adjunct labor, even as tenured faculty's primary work is teaching, simply because their adjunct per course wages tend to be so low. This is evidence of why we must significantly increase funding to community colleges.

QUESTION: In an effort to achieve a surface-level equity

around pay for teaching labor, couldn't institutions (arbitrarily) declare that some smaller proportion of all tenured faculty's salaries are earmarked for teaching, thus driving down the per course wage?

ANSWER: Sure, but in my scenario, even if the tenurable faculty go down to 20 percent of their job being teaching-related, the lecturers and adjuncts would see sizable increases over their current wage. I also believe that any system in which the institution is funded through a combination of federal and state money in lieu of tuition will require all faculty, regardless of status and rank, to teach as a reasonably significant portion of their labor.

In this scenario, the vast majority of laborers will see improved conditions because every position will come with an equitable wage. It is possible that some faculty at the upper end would see a reduction in wages or a requirement to teach more than they do currently, but if funding that is earmarked for instruction is paying that wage, this is how it must be. More teaching should also come coupled with reduced expectations around research. Ending the prestige arm's race should have a positive effect on all faculty beyond the most rarified superstars, with the greatest positives being for those furthest down the rank ladder.

We know that the status quo is unsustainable and exploitive. It is not consistent with an institution of higher learning that is sustainable, resilient, and free. Faculty who want to get out of teaching will have to fund their own releases.

But paying a consistent wage for the same work should not seem utopian. That we seem far from achieving this is mostly a testament to how much slippage we've allowed over the last three decades.

It really isn't complicated. Equal pay for equal work.

CHAPTER 10

The Other Work of Faculty:
Tenure, Governance, Inclusion

The structure of how labor is valued and compensated is only part of what we must consider when it comes to the faculty of sustainable, resilient, and free public colleges and universities. We must also consider how faculty go about their work, which means examining issues of tenure, shared governance and administration, and, of course, the question of who is allowed through the gates of academia to begin with.

Tenure Is Already Dead

In recent years, we've seen a near constant assault on faculty tenure rights by state legislatures. Tennessee, Wisconsin, Kentucky, and Arkansas have all taken explicit steps to weaken the rights of faculty who have earned tenure. Iowa and Missouri have made similar attempts but ultimately didn't get far, though even their proposals to essentially eliminate tenure protections would have been unthinkable just a decade ago.

In appealing to the Tennessee system board in 2018 to forgo a policy change that many viewed as a "stealth attempt to chip away at tenure," University of Tennessee professor Marcia Black "cast tenure as an essential protection, a tenet of democracy, the foundation of academic freedom. It's what allows professors to teach, write, or do research that challenges the status quo without fearing reprisal."[1]

It is a stirring defense of tenure that is, unfortunately, not true.

For college instructors who labor not only without tenure, but also on year-to-year (or even semester-to-semester) contracts, tenure was never alive in the first place. And as this describes the majority of college faculty who teach now, it is difficult to see how tenure can be truly essential to a college's or university's operation. I personally have twenty years of classroom experience. I worked every one of those years without the benefit of tenure, with a contract that ended at the end of the academic year. For the large majority of people who work in public higher education, tenure is not an "essential protection"—it is a job perk.

The reason for this comes down to the difference between what I call "tenure as a principle" and "tenure as a policy." Tenure as a principle works precisely how Professor Black described it to the Tennessee board; it allows faculty members to do their work to the best of their ability. It protects faculty so they can participate in shared governance and pursue their research without falling afoul of administrative or political disfavor. The notion that institutional and intellectual work done in good faith should be protected is a good one, an "essential" one even. The problem is that most faculty do not have these protections. And when that happens, the collective power of the entire faculty is diminished.

This reality has been particularly stark during the pandemic, as faculty have been essentially reduced to writing pleading letters to administrations and boards in an attempt to shape institutional policies around the coronavirus. In many (but by no means all) cases, tenured faculty have been given some measure of personal autonomy—for example, the freedom to choose to hold their own classes remotely—but as a collective body, they have had little to no control over the actual operations of the institution. In many cases, they don't even seem to have any *influence* over administrations.

This is a clear sign that "tenure as a principle" has become "tenure as a policy." It is something to be doled out to the elect, which has allowed for the establishment of a multitiered faculty system where only the top tier has access to the protections of "tenure as a principle." And because decisions about the destruction of tenure ultimately lie with administrators, tenure has now become an instrument of administrative control; administrators and governing boards wield all the power of any significance.

Tenure as a principle was conceived without knowledge or foresight of a future of tenure as a policy. Tenure as a policy is a state of affairs that has emerged gradually as a consequence of the corporatized university. It is not the fault of faculty who are currently tenured, though we should recognize that these trends have been developing over decades and that taking steps to arrest them earlier might have left faculty in a better position now.

Tenure as a policy harms tenured faculty by increasing their responsibilities and workload. By making those eligible for the status increasingly scarce, over time, more burdens fall on those who remain. Tenure's scarcity also creates an atmosphere where actually "using" the protections that come with it is a risky practice. Over the years, I have heard from many tenured faculty about how powerless they truly feel because of their limited numbers, which makes them hesitant to wield whatever power they may still possess.

As we've seen, tenure as a policy especially harms nontenure faculty. It ensures that they work for less money in more precarious positions and that they are shut out from the academic freedom protections that an even watered-down tenure system provides. During the pandemic, many tenured faculty have suddenly become acquainted with the conditions under which nontenure faculty have been working for years. In the face of dire financial exigency, tenure is no protection for anyone.

The current system of tenure is neither sustainable nor resilient. In fact, it is melting away as surely and inexorably as

Greenland's ice sheet. There is no hope in reclaiming what is lost. And so we must adapt to what remains.

The Post-Tenure University

I have no wish to end tenure, and if I had my druthers, I would simply make all faculty positions tenure-eligible.[2] But we should also admit that tenure by itself is not up to the job we believe it is designed to do. If it was, the erosions of its power wouldn't have happened in the first place.

So what kind of solution is up to the job?

Achieving wage equity is one important piece of this puzzle. If we eliminate the rationale for colleges and universities to hire contingent laborers as a way to reduce costs, the incentive to increase the proportion of adjunct laborers will be eliminated. The additional federal aid that will allow institutions to become tuition-free should come coupled with requirements around wages and labor, including the establishment of maximum thresholds for the number of part-time contingent or adjunct faculty a college or university is allowed to employ.[3]

In response, schools could create full-time positions that exist outside of the tenure stream as a way to free themselves of the burden of having faculty with job protections. The idealist in me hopes that by resetting our institutions around mission and pedagogy, rather than around revenue and operations, we will see this mentality decline or disappear. There is no doubt that the quality of instruction benefits from the maximum continuity of faculty. If we believe this, maybe colleges and universities can live by the values they espouse.

However, the pragmatist in me realizes that because of what has happened with tenure as a principle, it's better to have actual concrete rules in place. In that sense, there really is only one solution. Colleges and universities must establish a floor of rights that apply to all faculty who are laboring as part of the mission of teaching and learning. Those rights should include an end of at-will employment and the institution of affirmative academic freedom protections for all faculty and staff.

By acknowledging that teaching is the core labor of instructional workers at colleges and universities, by acknowledging the conditions under which people do their best work and then seeking to achieve those conditions, institutions will benefit. This also requires faculty to reclaim the power they have ceded to administrators and to reduce, and even eliminate, the divide between faculty and administration that currently defines higher education.

A Return of Shared Governance

I do not believe in the trope of the "evil administrator," the dean, provost, or president who simply has it in for faculty and will do everything in their power to make faculty more and more miserable. Those types of administrators may exist, but in my experience, they are rare.

While there are no doubt administrative decisions that baffle and frustrate faculty—and some of the institutional leadership around the coronavirus pandemic seems downright disastrous—it's important to acknowledge these issues are almost entirely attributable to the structural and systemic problems I've outlined elsewhere in this book. The leaders of public colleges and universities have been tasked with managing their institutions through a long period of austerity and decline while simultaneously being required to present a public face of success. In reality, it is impossible to "do more with less," and yet if one is going to take on the responsibility of higher education administration, this is exactly what they have been attempting to do.

That task's impossibility has created inevitable tensions. Faculty and staff believe they need things; and the administrator's job is to say "no." And as more and more of the institutional work at colleges and universities moves away from "governance" and toward "management," the responsibilities and power of administrators increase. Faculty are marginalized because what they have to offer does not apply to the problems of managing austerity. Consequently, over time, faculty and administrative interests diverge, even as both groups are entirely dedicated to the institution's success in their own ways.

I hope that by eliminating the chase for revenue and removing the yoke of austerity, the gap between administrations and faculty will close a bit. In the long term, though, institutions must embrace not just a return to robust shared governance,[4] but a model that relies on faculty administrators. Everyone in administration should also teach, and all those who primarily teach should have a voice and role in administration. Colleges and universities should also consider adopting a structure where administrative roles—above and beyond the position of department chair—rotate on a consistent basis. Experience and continuity are important aspects of good leadership. But an organization in which everyone is a potential future leader, and where leaders may again find themselves among the nonmanagerial class, will be structured more readily to operate according to a school's deeper institutional values.

Balancing the salaries among these roles to eliminate the corporate "executive class" structure of our current institutions would also have positive benefits. Rather than being the sole guaranteed route to an increased salary in the world of higher education, administrative work should be more explicitly tied to the authentic desire to serve the institution.

There are likely other structures and policies that could be beneficial to fulfilling the mission of public colleges and universities, but the core principles must remain central at all times—mission over operations; everyone with a stake gets a say.

Once that's taken care of, the next question to consider is who is allowed inside the institution to have that say.

Diversity and the Pipeline Problem

A sustainable public college or university that is largely funded by public funds should reflect the public it serves. Currently, however, there is a gap between the representation of different groups inside the university and their presence in the populace at large. As the Association of American Colleges and Universities put it in their 2019 report on the demographics in higher education, "College students are more diverse than ever. Faculty and administrators are not."[5]

Nationwide, only about 6 percent of faculty are Black, compared to 14 percent of students.[6] This is true despite many years of public concern over the lack of representation among college faculty. This is often characterized as a problem with the faculty "pipeline"—the suggestion that it is difficult to recruit and retain Black scholars who meet the tenure standards at academic institutions.

You will often hear about the problem of a "lack of candidates" in industries that lack diversity. For example, there has long been a problem of diversity and representation in the late-night comedy writing ranks, which is often chalked up to a pipeline problem. The places where those candidates could be found—Second City and the Groundlings, for example—had very few women members. Sometimes, when a new position opened up, not a single woman would apply. And if someone doesn't apply, they can't be hired.

I learned some things about the nature of pipelines from 2003 to 2008, when I was the keeper of the pipeline for a much smaller comedic property than a late-night television show—the humor website *McSweeney's Internet Tendency*—but one that was seeking out contributors from the same pool of talent nonetheless.[7] Rather than a feeder system of improv troupes and the *Harvard Lampoon*, my pipeline was an email inbox.

In the earliest days of my tenure there, it was sometimes tough to find material I considered good enough to publish. I leaned on past contributors pretty heavily, but as our audience increased, so did the traffic to my inbox for submissions. I noticed a few things:

> 1. At the start, men counted for between 70 to 80 percent of the submissions.

> 2. Upon receiving a rejection, men were much more inclined to follow up with another submission, sometimes almost immediately.[8]

> 3. While women were a much smaller percentage of the total submissions, they had a much higher likelihood of acceptance.

> 4. Women who had received a rejection were much less likely to resubmit right away, and sometimes would not resubmit at all.

On the surface, unlike more prominent comedy entities, *McSweeney's Internet Tendency* had an egalitarian pipeline. I didn't care what your background was, who you'd interned for, or where you took improv classes—I was starved for content. But even that egalitarian pipeline wasn't doing the job by itself.

Please recognize, I am not championing myself as some contender for gold in the equity Olympics. I had no explicit goal to achieve diversity at *McSweeney's Internet Tendency*. I only wanted to ease my own burden over having to relentlessly seek out funny content, and women were an underutilized source in that pursuit.

I made one small change. After reflecting on the lower

rates of resubmission among women, I started writing short (and I mean short) bits of encouragement to those writers who really had gotten close to acceptance. At the same time, I—let's just go with "hounded"—our existing female contributors for more material.

Over time, the percentage of submissions by women increased. Many writers who had been rejected initially ultimately landed material on the site and subsequently became consistent contributors. In 2019, seventeen of the site's twenty most-read pieces were authored or coauthored by women. And in 2020, women make up a majority of the site's contributors.[9] Something else interesting happened as well. By all possible metrics—traffic, cultural influence, revenue—the site is performing better each year. The increased diversity has made for a superior product. The material published at *McSweeney's Internet Tendency* reflects a broader array of experiences than it did fifteen or twenty years ago, and it is better for it.

One of the unspoken assumptions of the pipeline problem that must be challenged is not just about who gets into the pipeline at the start, but what the "standards" are that govern the flow of people through it. In comedy, the assumption for years was that there just weren't enough women who were up to snuff as measured against the dominant white guy, the guy who fit the *Harvard Lampoon* staffing ethos that predominated in elite outlets. And when a pipeline's default framework goes unquestioned, some people who merit inclusion will undoubtedly be judged as falling short simply because of their differences from that default.

This is particularly true in academia.

When Excellence Looks Different
The spring 2020 semester delivered an object lesson in what happens when higher education's longstanding procedures and policies are not designed to handle or recognize excellence

when it comes in an unfamiliar package.

Paul Harris, an assistant professor of human services with research specialties in Black male student athletes and underrepresented students' college readiness, was denied tenure by the University of Virginia. This was a surprise. All of Dr. Harris's pretenure reviews had shown him meeting or exceeding the standards for tenure and promotion. A graduate of UVA himself, Harris had even served as a live-in residential life supervisor with his wife—the writer Taylor Harris— and their two young children. UVA had also made a public commitment to recruiting and retaining more faculty of color.

The summary of Harris's appeal[10] shows a number of disconnects between the work he'd been doing and how it was judged by his reviewers and the tenure committee, however. For example, some of his publications that appeared in refereed journals were classified by reviewers as "self-published." It is clear his reviewers did not fully understand and appreciate the context of Dr. Harris's scholarship. He studies populations that have long been ignored using methods uniquely designed for his scholarship and subjects; his work exists outside the default framework.

In justifying their initial denial, UVA consistently cited the "objective" review of all candidates for tenure. Rather than serving as a defense, this response was the tell, the university's admission that the very features on which they rested their decisions were simply the nature of the so-called pipeline problem.

White scholars working in new territory are allowed to be geniuses. Black ones are "different," or even inferior, when they're judged against that same "objective" criteria. At the time of Harris's denial, I joked on Twitter that if Miles Davis had been an academic and had submitted *Bitches Brew* for his tenure and promotion diary, he would've been rejected.

Harris did not look like the tenure applicants who had

come before him, and therefore he could not be worthy of tenure. All of this could happen without any ill-intent or overt prejudice on the part of the review committee members. The bias was baked in.

Achieving diversity requires an admission that your previous definition of "excellence" may not be expansive enough. If the only way for a Black scholar to achieve tenure is to emulate the work of the white, structural majority, higher education will never realize a representative proportion of Black scholars. Colleges and universities will have failed at achieving diversity, but more importantly, they will have failed to truly strive for excellence.

After a noisy public campaign, including a hashtag (#tenureforpaul), a petition, and a widely read personal essay by Taylor Harris,[11] herself a UVA alumna, the denial was reversed, and Dr. Paul Harris was tenured by the University of Virginia.

Remarking on what the university learned through the process, Bob Pianta, Dean at the Curry School of Education and Human Development, wrote in a letter:

> One realization for me was the importance of our reviews reflecting a broad view of scholarly impact, particularly in emerging fields. I also gained a deeper understanding of the impact of community-engaged scholarship, particularly when involved with questions of relevance to marginalized groups, and the important role that community-engaged scholarship plays in describing, identifying, and elevating assets of such groups.[12]

In other words, Pianta knows a bunch of stuff he wasn't aware of before. Isn't this the mission of education writ large?

There are no doubt many other cases like Harris's that slip

by without notice, where promising scholars are denied the chance to contribute to and shape the contours of academia. Our sustainable and resilient colleges and universities of the future must make room for voices that exist outside the default. They also must make room for all of the voices that make up our institutions of higher education while navigating a culture that is increasingly hostile to the very existence of those same institutions.

CHAPTER 11

Navigating the Culture Wars

L adies and gentlemen, the president of the United States:

> Ironically, on the 200th anniversary of our Bill of Rights, we find free speech under assault throughout the United States, including on some college campuses. The notion of political correctness has ignited controversy across the land. And although the movement arises from the laudable desire to sweep away the debris of racism and sexism and hatred, it replaces old prejudice with new ones. It declares certain topics off-limits, certain expression off-limits, even certain gestures off-limits.

Any institution is in trouble when the president of the United States comes for it, which means colleges and universities are in a difficult spot.

In 2012, 2015, 2017, and 2019, the Pew Research Center surveyed Americans about their attitudes toward higher education, asking if "colleges and universities have a positive or negative effect of the way things are going in this country."[1] In 2012 and 2015, self-identified Democrats were more positively disposed toward colleges and universities than self-identified Republicans, but even Republicans expressed an overall net positive sentiment. By 2017, however, something happened:

The most obvious proximate cause of this inversion is the election of Donald Trump, but there's a deeper story about how colleges and universities went from being an antagonist for Republicans that was still (somewhat grudgingly) accepted, to instead being viewed as an outright enemy of the state. It also tells us something about how sustainable and resilient colleges and universities will best be able to deal with inevitable culture war flare-ups in the future.

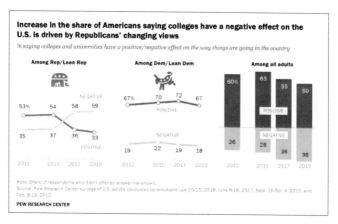

Increase in the share of Americans saying colleges have a negative effect on the U.S. is driven by Republicans' changing views

% saying colleges and universities have a positive/negative effect on the way things are going in the country

Note: Share of respondents who didn't offer an answer not shown.
Source: Pew Research Center surveys of U.S. adults conducted by telephone July 10-15, 2019. June 8-18, 2017. Sept. 16-Oct. 4, 2015, and Feb. 8-12, 2015.

PEW RESEARCH CENTER

Right-Wing "Watchdogs"

In 2016, Turning Point USA, a conservative nonprofit founded in 2012 by then-nineteen-year-old Charlie Kirk, launched its "Professor Watchlist." The website itself was (and is) comically inept, but it ultimately became a calling card for Kirk's entry into Trump administration circles. Between 2016 and 2019, Turning Point USA's revenues have climbed from $4.3 million to $28.5 million a year. Kirk's annual salary has increased over that same period from $27,231 to $292,423, proving that you absolutely don't need a college degree to make a decent living.[2] But at least in Kirk's case, you do need colleges, because otherwise he wouldn't have a bogeyman to rail and fundraise against.

Historically, a figure like Kirk shouldn't cause too much worry for higher education institutions. The charge that universities are hostile to conservatives and conservative thought is as old as universities themselves, and the ritual of a young conservative attacking higher education is renewed with each subsequent generation, as seen in William F. Buckley Jr.'s *God and Man at Yale* (1951) and Ross Douthat's *Privilege: Harvard and the Education of the Ruling Class* (2005). But while the right's general approval of higher education institutions has always been lower than the rest of the public, the idea that colleges and universities were somehow actively harmful to the country as a whole was a position held only by a distinct minority.

This cultural narrative was generally fixed in place, until it was deliberately pried loose. In addition to Turning Point USA, recent years have seen the rise of conservative-oriented websites such as the *College Fix* and *Campus Reform*, deliberately written from a point of view antagonistic to higher education. *Campus Reform* solicits stories from students themselves, framing them as first-person exposés of professorial leftist extremism.

Undoubtedly, Trump's ascendance, and his brand of white identity politics, which is predicated on an existential fight against enemies, has inflamed sentiments on the right. That these politics are amplified by publications dedicated to seeding misinformation into the social media bloodstream is a significant problem. But I still believe these sentiments would have remained a minority opinion, even in the Republican Party, if it had not been for some help from another source.

In 2015, a handful of campus incidents received widespread, mainstream, negative media coverage in a relatively short period of time, all of it coalescing around a narrative of college students being a "coddled" group made up of "snowflakes," young people incapable of productively dealing with differences of opinion or emotional challenges on their campuses. Writing at the *New York Times*, Judith Shulevitz assailed Brown University for offering students so-called "safe spaces" as an alternative to a planned campus program on rape and sexual assault.[3] Students at Oberlin were pilloried for allegedly complaining that an inauthentic dining hall sandwich labeled as a banh mi was "cultural appropriation."[4] And at Yale, an incident over communications from administrators regarding culturally offensive Halloween costumes went viral, with students shouting at Nicholas Christakis, a Yale professor and one of the campus house "masters," that it was his job to "create a place of comfort and home for the students who live in Silliman [a Yale residence]." When Christakis disagreed, a student shouted, as part of a hail of profanities, that he should "step down" if he was unwilling to do this.[5]

That same year saw the publication of an article in the *Atlantic,* "The Coddling of the American Mind,"[6] by NYU sociologist Jonathan Haidt, and Greg Lukianoff, president of the Foundation for Individual Rights in Education, a libertarian-oriented campus watchdog. The article explicitly argued that students' mental health was being harmed by practices such as "safe spaces" and "trigger warnings." In Haidt and Lukianoff's 2018 book of the same title, they declared there was a full-blown culture, called "safetyism," that was contributing to poor mental health among college students and eroding higher education's ability to fulfill its core mission. In these stories, we see an important distinction from the right-wing critiques of liberal professors brainwashing students. These narratives suggest that it is the students themselves who are undermining the work of the institution.

The cultural narrative of dysfunction and damage had escaped the Right and spread to the Center and Center-Left, finding a welcoming home at publications that were far removed from the *College Fix*. At the *Atlantic*, staff contributor Conor Friedersdorf became a self-appointed defender of the principles of the academy, weighing in on just about every public incident that occurred there. It became something of a cottage industry among center-left academics to wring their hands over this trend. The book version of *The Coddling of the American Mind* became a best seller and was widely accepted as a diagnosis, by ostensibly credible observers, of what ails us.

A search of US news sources indexed in the ProQuest database confirms the virality of these narratives. Mentions of the term "snowflakes" in reference to college students doubled from 2016 to 2017. Mentions of the term "coddled" in the same context tripled between 2014 and 2016.

In hindsight, it is interesting to note that much of the instant outrage over these incidents was overblown, based on inaccurate reporting, and missing crucial context. The cultural narrative did not reflect the real story. Unfortunately, this skewed cultural narrative had much more power and influence than the truth when it came to shaping the public's perception of colleges and universities.

Writing for the *Chronicle of Higher Education* in 2019, Vimal Patel rereported the infamous banh mi incident at Oberlin, finding that it was fundamentally misreported and then further skewed and amplified by the *New York Post*—under the headline, "Students at Lena Dunham's College Offended by Lack of Fried Chicken"—more than a month after the initial occurrence. The *New York Times*, *Newsweek*, the *Washington Post*, and the *Atlantic* had then weighed in with takes of their own, amplifying the narrative many times over. Like a children's game of telephone, each repetition distorted reality a bit more until all that was left was a core narrative about hypersensitive, politically correct students run amok.

The events surrounding the Yale Halloween costume incident also took on a different light following the release of a "devastating account"[7] of an internal report on Yale's enabling of a "climate hostile to many female and minority professors" and an atmosphere that was unwelcoming to minority students. The media had recorded numerous incidents of outright hostility expressed toward minority students in the period prior to the Halloween night incident.[8] The original letter written by Erika Christakis, which some students saw as a defense of the rights of nonminority students to dress up in minstrelized versions of people from other cultures, and which triggered the unrest, had come in the wake of a previous administration missive that asked students to consider others in their choice of costumes. The student outrage was over a betrayal that felt personal, as the house masters—who are indeed tasked with supporting the well-being of students— seemed to choose an abstract (and frankly silly) defense of "free speech" over the desires of nonwhite students to not see their identities used for the purposes of cheap entertainment.

The outrage on that night appeared to be rooted in much deeper problems than a single dispute over Halloween costumes. It was years of frustration at being excluded finally boiling over, a fundamentally different story than the one about students running roughshod over administrators and demanding a "safe space." But the news of Yale's report of a campus hostile to nonwhite faculty and students was confined to higher education circles at best, and as we've seen, the narrative surrounding issues of faculty recruitment and diversity are complex. But on the other hand, the narrative of "coddled" college students was easily received by audiences who had been primed to believe it.

The inversion in Republican sentiment toward colleges and universities is currently having obvious negative consequences. There is little hunger to provide the kinds of funds institutions need to manage their way through the pandemic. In conservative states such as North Carolina, colleges and universities are at times treated with outright hostility by governing boards larded with conservative activists. But this hostility has been compounded by centrist, and even some liberal, academics who are using an ostensible defense of bedrock principles to cloak what looks like a desire to protect their institutional turf from challenges to their authority.

The horses are so far out of the barn on this problem that you can't even see their hoofprints. But this doesn't mean we can ignore the problem and just hope it goes away.

Reclaiming the Narrative

In December of 1964, Mario Savio stood on the steps of the student center at the University of California, Berkeley and directly challenged university President Clark Kerr to do more for the cause of civil rights on campus. Savio rallied students to throw their "bodies upon the gears" of the machinery standing in the way of racial equality. Somehow, despite this challenge to authority, the republic still stands.[9] Kerr remains as one of the most legendary figures in higher education.

Clashes between students and administrators are not new. In fact, they are endemic to the operation of colleges and universities, which should be places of productive conflict and progress. Remember that statement at the beginning of this chapter from the president of the United States decrying the scourge of political correctness? That wasn't Donald Trump. It was George H. W. Bush, speaking at the University of Michigan commencement in May of 1991.[10]

One of the core values that colleges and universities must embrace is students' fundamental right to self-expression and the exercise of their First Amendment rights. A student yelling "Who the fuck hired you?" at Nicholas Christakis, the Yale house master, is not an example of "bullying," as it was characterized by Conor Friedersdorf. It's discourse.[11]

Sure, it may not be the most productive discourse, but the hand-wringing and pearl clutching by ostensibly liberal academics or cultural commentators about the direct confrontation by students who were advocating for a campus climate in which they could be heard calls into question exactly who has been coddled on campuses. Is there a more sensitive creature than the tenured professor at an elite institution?

One of the problems of a corporatized university that uses a student-as-customer model is the tension over that old saw that the "customer is always right." Colleges and universities present themselves as willing, and even eager, to cater to student needs as a sales pitch for tuition dollars, but when students protest and state what they want, those very same institutions label their actions as something that goes beyond the bounds of acceptable behavior.

We must allow our institutions of higher education to be absolutely as contentious as necessary so that all points of view can be heard. When injustices are identified, they should be addressed, but if administrations believe that students are making unreasonable demands, they must stand on principle, rather than concerning themselves with needing to respond to the desires of the customer.

At the sustainable, resilient, and free university, I *hope* there will be conflicts; these conflicts are often the very things that move our institutions forward. Protests from Yale students resulted in the removal of the name of John C. Calhoun—one of history's great monsters—from one of its residence halls. That argument was an important precursor to the removal of other monuments to Calhoun in the aftermath of the summer 2020 marches for social justice across the country.

Students are not a group to be feared on campus if they are treated with the respect any stakeholder deserves. That collective group of stakeholders, it should go without saying, also includes conservatives. Fortunately, conservatives are already doing fine.

Being Conservative on Campus
Those of us who have worked at public institutions can become easily frustrated by charges that faculty are a bunch

of "intersectional Marxist critical theorists who hate America," a cabal working to indoctrinate students. We know firsthand how absurd the charge is.

The reality is that the vast majority of instructional faculty deeply believe in fostering student self-development, and they have no wish to create clones of themselves through their teaching. One of postsecondary education's highest callings is its role in exposing students to perspectives different from their own so they may then re-form their personal critical sensibility. The most fulfilling part of my job as a teacher of writing is seeing students empowered to become who they are on the page. While I strongly desire they practice the values associated with writing carefully for the benefit of an intended audience, the underlying opinions they express while practicing those values are largely immaterial to me.

For the majority of my career, I have been a outlier in my own classroom, a northerner in the South, a non-believer among the devoutly faithful. These differences are the source of opportunities for learning, rather than something to be feared. The evidence suggests that in the vast majority of cases, this is exactly what is happening.

Study after study, many of them conducted by conservative faculty themselves, shows that professors are not, in fact, indoctrinating their students. According to the *Study of American Families and General Social Survey*, attending college shifts American students' attitudes around civil liberties, but it has no effect on their political orientation.[12] Another study found that while college students grew more liberal over their four years in school, the change was indistinguishable from that experienced by noncollege attendees of the same age.[13] Peers are the primary influence on the social and political attitudes of college students, which makes sense given the far greater amount of time students spend embedded in these groups compared to their exposure to faculty.[14]

I could list numerous other studies[15] supporting my claim, but the reality is that for many people, there is no amount of evidence that would dissuade them from their belief that colleges and universities are a fifth column that hates America. Even for those who don't feel quite this strongly, it is difficult to imagine a world where there is not at least some suspicion directed at a faculty body that overwhelmingly identifies as liberal.

Even this notion of an overwhelmingly "liberal" faculty can be called into question, though. In what still is today the most complete survey of professorial politics, because it actually includes community college instructors, we find that while conservatives are a distinct minority (9.2 percent), moderates are the largest group (46.1 percent).[16] Other studies have found large variations by field of study, or even region. There is likewise little evidence, beyond the anecdotal, that conservative students are discriminated against in graduate admissions or the hiring process; much of that imbalance is simply related to self-selection. Conservative students are also not graded more harshly or unfairly than liberal students.[17] According to *Passing on the Right: Conservative Professors in the Progressive University*, once conservatives are on campus, they report being generally contented with how they've been treated. A greater proportion of conservative professors say they'd do their academic career all over again (66 percent) than liberal professors (56 percent).[18]

Ultimately, there is little doubt that campuses in general are predominantly populated by people with liberal views, but there is no evidence that they are inherently hostile to conservatives.

But Really, What Should We Do?

There is no need for colleges and universities to be caught flat-footed by controversies that crop up regularly, especially when there are plenty of previous examples from which schools can draw important lessons on how to effectively respond to them. PEN America, for example, has compiled a handy list of resources for institutions to draw upon, including advice for faculty who are being brigaded by online harassment, or actions an institution can take if it is dealing with calls to fire a faculty member over an act of speech.[19]

Because of the nature of our social media ecosystem and the presence of less-than-good-faith actors like Charlie Kirk and the *Campus Fix*, there will be many ginned-up controversies that can easily be weathered. It's just a matter of making sure every institution has built up a resiliency to this sort of attack. Part of that resiliency stems from the ability to discern between a good-faith controversy, which requires community engagement, and bad-faith outrage. It is not particularly difficult to respond to any potentially inflammatory speech act with a boilerplate response: "As part of our institution's commitment to academic freedom, we do not comment on the speech of faculty, staff, or students that is protected by the First Amendment." This allows the— often nongenuine—outrage posse to move on, while also giving time to investigate what happened and to see if there is any role for the institution to play.

That resiliency also stems from colleges and universities genuinely respecting student voices and student autonomy. If students believe that they are being listened to and respected, they will collaborate on solutions rather than demanding satisfaction as customers.

It would also help for colleges and universities to simply be a little nimbler. Take Oberlin, for example, a unique institution of a genuinely progressive orientation that is no more typical of how colleges operate on one side of the political spectrum than Liberty University is on the other. Oberlin need not apologize for being itself as long as it is also putting the affirmative story of the school and its legacy into the world. In response to bad-faith critiques, Oberlin's response can be simple and straightforward: "There they are, using old Oberlin as a convenient punching bag again. Meanwhile, are you familiar with our four Nobel Laureates, our more than a dozen Grammy/Tony/Emmy winners, and our baker's dozen of MacArthur Genius Grant recipients? And yeah, Lena Dunham too."

But here's the more important thing for public higher education institutions. They need to stop letting themselves be defined by what goes on at elite private institutions. Public institutions have a different story to tell, one that I believe will change how the work of public higher education is perceived in the culture more broadly, and that will hopefully engender greater support. And one of the reasons this is a superior story is because it happens to be true.

PART IV
RENEWAL

CHAPTER 12

Students Are Not the Enemy

Safetyism was never real.

Launched into the world by Haidt and Lukianoff in *The Coddling of the American Mind*, the term "refers to a culture or belief system in which safety has become a sacred value, which means that people are unwilling to make trade-offs demanded by other practical and moral concerns." According to the authors, safetyism—along with other factors such as "screen time"[1]—was causing observable increases in anxiety and depression among young people. It was also leading to protests, such as the one at Yale over Halloween costumes, which the authors see as an illiberal assault on one of higher education's core values.

Safetyism, the idea of "coddling," and the characterization of students as "snowflakes" are all attempts to pathologize responses and worldviews that, in many cases, are the product of differences that are rooted in specific experiences of the world. They are examples of the time immemorial activity of older generations finding fault with younger ones; the difference this time is that the criticism is couched as an actual mental disorder that poses a threat to liberalism.[2]

I am trying to reconcile the description of a generation so apparently fragile that it cannot even bear a challenging thought with the images of young people who have also faced pepper spray, tear gas, beatings, and rubber bullets on the streets as they have protested systemic injustice in the wake of the killings of George Floyd, Breonna Taylor, Ahmaud Arbery, and others. I'm seeing plenty of bravery, a sense of sacrifice rooted in anger, frustration, despair, and desperation. I'm not seeing any safetyism.

If safetyism is a thing, its true avatar is President Donald Trump. His first act after his inauguration was to send his press secretary out to lie about the size of the crowds on the National Mall. In June 2020, peaceful protesters near the White House were teargassed so that the president could stage a photo op in front of a church holding a Bible. Trump's inability to withstand even the slightest criticism without lashing out is a hallmark of his presidency. It has largely been normalized as a matter of his style or politics, rather than pathologized as Haidt and Lukianoff do with the members of Generation Z, but the pattern is clear.

New York Times columnist Bret Stephens (like me, a Gen-Xer) is another example of someone who has decried the pernicious influence of safetyism while cocooning himself in a protective bubble of status. In a 2017 commencement address at Hampden-Sydney College, Stephens criticized the existence of so-called safe spaces on campuses, ultimately exhorting students to:

> get out of your own safe spaces. Define what your intellectual comfort zone is—and leave it. Enhance your tolerance for discordant voices. Narrow your criteria for what's beyond the pale. Read the authors or watch the talking heads with whom you disagree. Treat those disagreements as a whetting stone to sharpen your own arguments. Resist the temptation to call people names.[3]

In 2019, after David Karpf, a professor at George Washington University, joked about Stephens being a metaphoric "bedbug" at the *New York Times*—at the time, the newspapers's offices were being afflicted by the actual pests—an offended Stephens emailed both Karpf and a GWU provost in what can only be read as an attempt to use his platform to intimidate Karpf.[4]

When this failed to yield the desired results, Stephens wrote an entire column as an ex post facto justification over his hurt feelings, arguing (sans evidence) that Karpf's bedbug reference was inherently anti-Semitic and implying that Karpf (who is Jewish) had Nazi sympathies.[5] How's that for not calling someone names? Following the contretemps, Stephens accepted an invitation to debate Karpf at GWU, but later canceled when his insistence that the event be closed to the public was rejected.[6]

The reason neither Donald Trump nor Bret Stephens are tagged as practicing safetyists is solely because they hold positions of power and influence. In fact, if you examine those who wield the charge of safetyism against others, they are always in positions of superior power, accusing those without power of disrupting some important principle that protects the status quo. It's a good gig if you can get it. While holding all the cards, you get to tell others that they're not playing the game correctly.

When the disputes involve the academy, it is easy to look like a high-minded defender of the liberal order who is educating the leaders of tomorrow. Haidt and Lukianoff frame *Coddling* as an approach to help young people better cope with the world. That those young people may have a clearer understanding of the world than their well-credentialed elders does not seem to cross their minds. But given the trajectory of the country since those Yale students protested on Halloween amidst a broader climate of racial hostility, one wonders if maybe we could have avoided some of our current strife if we'd listened to them much earlier.

I do not doubt Haidt and Lukianoff's motivations, but I question the narrowness of their lens, and I lament the impact of their injecting "safetyism" into the discussion around generational change and political discourse. Safetyism has never been real. It is simply a clever word a couple smart guys coined to try to describe some behaviors by others that they didn't like. It was couched in the need to preserve values like "truth" and "free inquiry," but it has far more frequently been used to dismiss and silence the concerns of those without power who have been trying to alert the rest of us to the kinds of systemic problems that have come to a head and are currently roiling the nation.

A Culture of Scarcity and Precarity

At the time *The Coddling of the American Mind* was published, I had a different theory about what was driving student unrest: rather than acting out of a culture of "safetyism," students were actually acting out from a problem of "precarity" and "scarcity."

Today, a traditional-age first-year college student was in early grade school when the global economy cratered in such a way that even rich people got scared for a little while. The resulting "recovery" only exacerbated most people's sense of scarcity and precarity as the fruits of the recovery accrued to smaller and smaller groups. And in the midst of a global pandemic, we now have an even more severe economic contraction. Just look around. As we witness the essential fragility of our food supply, our health care system, our public health institutions, our educational institutions, our governmental norms, our economic system, and potentially even our electoral system, I would suggest that precarity has always been a far greater threat than safetyism.[7]

Is it any surprise that these particular students have experienced trickle-down anxiety?

When *Coddling* came out, I observed that the people in the generation Haidt and Lukianoff were pathologizing as psychologically defective were instead acting rationally in a world where the road to success is narrow and where security, once it's achieved, is increasingly precarious. The attitudes of members of Generation Z have been forged in the wake of a historic global recession and a system of higher education marked by increasingly high tuition and ballooning student debt. The young people who were being criticized for lacking resilience had good reason to be on edge for economic concerns alone. Couple this with their recognition of the failure of past generations to deal with the systemic problems of racism, economic inequality, and climate change, and perhaps we can appreciate the source of their discontent. Young people, often without fully knowing it, were signaling the essential fragility and precariousness of our institutions more largely by pointing out that expressing a belief in values and norms is meaningless when it's not coupled with action.

Those who decry others for practicing safetyism while demanding safe spaces for themselves are an affront to the values Haidt and Lukianoff claim to be attempting to protect. Those who fall back on safetyism—and its cousin, "cancel culture"—as a core societal problem, even as police wantonly beat, gas, and shoot "less lethal" projectiles at citizens who are exercising their First Amendment rights of free speech and free assembly, demonstrate how narrow those concerns truly are.[8]

Challenging, Transparent, and Free

"Challenging," "Transparent," and "Free" are the three pillars of my personal pedagogy. I think they're pretty good ways of looking at the work students should engage in while they labor as part of a college or university.

College should be difficult, in a good way. In an interview, Cornel West once said something that I took to heart in my work as a college instructor:

> I want to be able to engage in the grand calling of a Socratic teacher, which is not to persuade and convince students, but to unsettle and unnerve and

maybe even unhouse a few students, so that they experience that wonderful vertigo and dizziness in recognizing at least for a moment that their world view rests on pudding, but then see that they have something to fall back on. It's the shaping and forming of critical sensibility. That, for me, is what the high calling of pedagogy really is.

Students should expect to have their worldviews challenged at college. They should expect to do difficult work. They should come out the other side with an increased sense of their own agency, a belief that they have control over their own fate and that they know their own mind. Students should be sound critical thinkers who know their own critical sensibilities, rather than being defined by "snow globe reasoning" tests like the Collegiate Learning Assessment. They should feel connected to their institution and the world beyond it.

The most current data suggests that school itself, rather than social media or a culture of safetyism, is the primary cause of student anxiety and depression. A 2018 survey from the American College Health Association found that two-thirds of students had "felt overwhelming anxiety" at least once in the last twelve months.[9] A 2019 Pew Research Center survey of teenagers found that they see anxiety and depression as the biggest problem their peers face (over bullying, drug addiction, and even poverty); 70 percent of those surveyed said it is a "major problem."[10] An overwhelming number of those surveyed (95 percent) expressed a desire for a "job or career they enjoy." Simultaneously, two-thirds said that they feel "a lot" of pressure to get good grades. A 2015 survey from the Yale Center for Emotional Intelligence found that 75 percent of the words students used to express their emotions toward school were negative—words like "stressed," "tired," and "bored."[11] And data on student engagement shows that the level of engagement drops every year from fifth to eleventh grade. By eleventh grade, more students report being "actively disengaged" (34 percent) than "engaged" (32 percent).[12]

For many students, school has become a fundamentally alienating activity. These students are defeated, not coddled. I've had students tell me that their first school-related anxiety attacks happened in grade school. In her recent book, *Can't Even: How Millennials Became the Burnout Generation*, Anne Helen Peterson, journalist and former college professor, shares dozens of testimonies of people from the millennial generation climbing on an academic treadmill in grade school and increasingly feeling like its one they will never escape.

The idea that students are defective or that they're not doing college correctly must be abandoned, and faculty and leadership must instead do more listening. Listening is not coddling. A course that is more attuned to the realities of what students are dealing with makes space for greater rigor than one that seeks to impose the instructor's will upon the students. And when students are no longer customers, and when the stakes of the pursuit of the credential are not so high, we will be better able to help students realize their potential.

One of the best ways to make sure a course is challenging is to practice total transparency. Colleges and universities should invite students to be explicitly involved in setting and shaping the values that inform the work they do on campus. This also is not coddling, but is instead an invitation to partnership and participation. Passivity is the enemy of learning. If we require students to be active participants in their own learning—choosing the journey that is meaningful to them rather than being acted upon by forces beyond their control—they will have a superior learning experience.

Students should also have the same protections of academic freedom as faculty. Their ideas should be taken seriously, even (or especially) if we disagree with them. When faculty or administrators disagree with students, that disagreement should be handled with respect and transparency. This does not mean capitulating to student demands. Conflict should be a starting point for progress, rather than something to be feared. The educations students receive belong to the students themselves, so they should be given sufficient ownership over that process.

And that starts with what they study.

CHAPTER 13

What Students Should Learn

QUESTION: What should students study in the sustainable and resilient public college or university? What should they major in?

ANSWER: Anything they want.

Next chapter.

QUESTION: No, seriously, how do we prepare students for the jobs of the twenty-first century?

ANSWER: *Sigh.*

While being well-prepared to enter the workforce should be a by-product of a college education, earning a specific credential to fit the immediate needs of the employment market is a mug's game, and not something colleges and universities should overconcern themselves with.[1] As Matt Reed, vice president of academic affairs at Brookdale Community College in New Jersey and fellow blogger at *Inside Higher Ed*, notes, "At a really fundamental level, the labor market is a political and economic issue, rather than an educational one."[2] Public higher education institutions cannot alter the macroeconomic landscape. In fact, they have very little influence on employment marketplaces at all.

I have long found the rhetoric around concepts like "jobs for the twenty-first century" curious. It assumes that the nature of work and employment is changing at breakneck speed as we hurtle into the unknown, while simultaneously expressing strong certainty that one should major in STEM fields and pursue very specific degrees with a high likelihood of postgraduate employment. If the future is truly unknown, why are we presuming that a degree in, I don't know, packaging sciences, is the best possible inoculation against change?

A question like this shows how reducing a university degree to the limited private good of a credential has hampered the discussion around what students should be *learning* as opposed to what they should be majoring in.

The energy around quantifying the "worth" of a major, as embodied in efforts like Bill Gates's Postsecondary Value Commission, are inevitably couched in the business language of "return on investment," which, in short, means money.[3] This is part of the larger mania for quantification and so-called "data-driven" decision-making. Because we *can* collect data about wages as they are related to students' majors, this is what must matter.

This is obviously a limited view of the value of an education, but even if we accept wage-to-major data as potentially meaningful, the reality is that there are too many holes in the data and too many confounding variables to truly understand the clear and direct relationship between major and wage.

Zachary Bleemer, an economics PhD candidate at the University of California, Berkeley, has focused a portion of his research on the factors that underly this data, and explains why the data, in many cases, is essentially meaningless.[4] For one, Bleemer notes that students do not choose their majors randomly, so any attempt to compare outcomes runs into a problem of selection bias. Engineering majors may have an already proven aptitude for the subject, making success in the major more likely than if we were to funnel as many students as possible toward the field. Additionally, when students choose majors, they may be expressing their future employment preferences, many of which may not involve salary concerns. If particular majors (such as economics) attract people who desire to maximize earnings—as opposed to something like lifestyle flexibility—then economics majors will have higher earnings for reasons that have nothing to do with their chosen field of study.

Perhaps more troubling, the data we have on wage-to-major statistics is not nearly as robust as those who are focused on this quantification project would like us to believe. Databases like payscale.com rely on self-reported data from self-selected alumni. Other attempts are limited to recent graduates (in the last two to four years), which fails to give a comprehensive view of a lifetime of earnings. While it's possible that STEM majors are more likely to land an initial high-paying job, it may be the liberal arts majors who are better able to adapt to a changing employment landscape. In fact, research indicates that salaries for liberal arts majors catch up to those for STEM majors over time. As the headline to one *New York Times* article put it, "engineers sprint but English majors endure."[5] Perhaps more importantly, though, as Bleemer points out, "Wages don't correspond one-to-one with quality of life."

The notion that we should use data that is both incomplete and inconsistent with a broad understanding of what it means to be a happy and thriving person in the world simply doesn't make sense. But in a world where public institutions are tuition-free, we won't have to constrain students' choices around the questions of which major is "worth the cost." The answer will be: "All of them."

What Should Students Learn?

We all have our biases on this question, and mine no doubt are rooted in my three humanities degrees (BA Rhetoric, MA Literature, MFA Creative Writing) and how they've prepared me for a career trajectory with an ever-shifting variety of challenges. When I finished my MFA, I hoped to spend a life writing short stories with subtle, but emotionally devastating, epiphanic moments *à la* Raymond Carver.

It didn't happen because, as it turns out, I am not an acknowledged master of the short story. But I have managed to cobble together a life as a writer over the last twenty-plus years by being adaptable. Twenty years ago, my first book (coauthored with Kevin Guilfoile) was a political satire novelty title done primarily in colored pencil. Now I am doing this. There have been seven other books in between. I now work as a senior analyst and communication strategist for a market research firm, and despite never having even taken calculus, I'm comfortable with all manner of quantitative and qualitative research design and analysis.

Somehow along the way, I learned to think a little bit. I learned how to observe the world and draw inferences from those observations and conclusions from those inferences, which is the core of all critical thinking. My first semester in graduate school, when I was asked to write a lengthy explication of Gerard Manley Hopkins's sonnet, "God's Grandeur," I did not know how to do it, but I figured it out. The same was true for a focus group report I wrote early on in my first foray in market research, as well as many other things I've tackled in my professional life, like a novel, or a book proposing a reimagined framework for public higher education.

The Association of American Colleges and Universities (AAC&U) has a good scaffold for what students should learn with its LEAP (Liberal Education and America's Promise) initiative.[6] The list focuses on high-impact practices and authentic assessments that are broadly consistent with the meaningful experiences captured in the Purdue-Gallup research on educational outcomes. Taken together, the criteria suggest a curriculum that allows for maximum student agency and involvement in their own educations.

Rather than choosing a random smattering of courses to fulfill broadly defined categories, students should be encouraged to make connections between their courses, integrating their learning along the way. The University of Virginia is attempting this with their "New College Curriculum," which frames general education courses as "literacies" and "disciplines" rather than simply categorizing courses by subject areas.[7] There are other interesting experiments happening around the country, such as Roanoke College's attempt to embed seven to ten writing courses in every student's curriculum, an initiative I am decidedly for.[8] My personal pet suggestion is to require a proportion of nonmajor courses to be taken each semester, rather than framing them as something to "get out of the way."

There is no single policy solution to this issue. The key is to start by rooting the process in the values we associate with learning and the experiences we know translate to meaningful, long-term outcomes.

The Proof Is in the Pudding

Here's an example of how I can judge if someone has benefited from their college education. They can take the following statement by Secretary of Education Betsy DeVos—"Children starting kindergarten this year face a prospect of having 65 percent of the jobs they will ultimately fill not yet having been created"—and show how it is 100 percent made-up bullshit.

Perhaps they could start with a little critical reflection and observation, thinking about jobs that exist today that have only recently been invented. Data scientist? Computer programmer? YouTuber? Influencer? While the specifics of how to perform these jobs may be different, none of them are "new." DaVinci was a data scientist. The first computer programmer is widely considered to be Ada Lovelace in 1842. A YouTuber performs in a new medium, but it is an awfully big stretch to say the job is "newly created" when people have made a living through attention-seeking for millennia. The mix of skills and competencies necessary to work inside a field may change—a journalist probably should learn podcasting these days—but the essence of the job is fundamentally the same.

Maybe the curious person could go to the Bureau of

Labor and Statistics and see what kind of work people do now, including some of these biggies: Retail (10 percent), Professional Services (13 percent), Leisure and Hospitality (10 percent), and State and Local Government (12 percent). Collectively, these four categories make up half of all jobs. Do we see things changing so much within these industries that jobs that have *not yet been created* will replace all of the existing jobs in these categories?

Perhaps they could go looking for mentions of DeVos's statistic in the media or academic publications. This might then turn up a reference from the *Guardian* in December 2018,[9] which sources the claim that "65 percent of children entering primary schools today will work in jobs and functions that don't currently exist" by citing something called the *Universities UK Report*. Chasing down that source, they would find the claim referenced in a 2016 report by the World Economic Forum, so they would go there.[10] Having not heard of the World Economic Forum, they could dig around the organization's publicly available information (merely a click or two away) and they would notice that it is a "public-private partnership" funded by companies such as Accenture, BlackRock, Boston Consulting, Credit Suisse, Goldman Sachs, Google, Facebook, and numerous others.

With their critical faculties kicking in, they would now be a little skeptical about the impartiality of this information, as the World Economic Forum appears to be a think tank funded by the world's largest corporations with a heavy concentration in banking and finance. Still, even corporation-funded think tanks can provide valid information, so they would find the specific reference in the report that declares, "by one popular estimate, 65 percent of children entering primary school today will ultimately end up working in job types that don't yet exist." The report credits this statement to a couple of folks named Scott McLeod and Karl Fisch for something titled "Shift

Happens," which has a URL of shifthappens.wikispaces.com. At last, the critically thinking person appears to be at the end of the game of internet telephone. But what do they find at shifthappens.wikispaces.com? A "file not found" message.

Uh-oh.

There appears to be no reliable extant source to support the claim that 65 percent of the jobs that kindergartners starting this year will hold have not yet been invented. The evidence for the claim that 65 percent of the jobs today's kindergarteners will have don't yet exist . . . doesn't exit. And yet, it has still taken root as a signal of disruption and something to hold over the heads of institutions to force them to be more responsive to the "market." Those who make the claim seem to be using it to promote a particular agenda related to the purpose and structure of education, namely that it should be "training" for the employment marketplace as opposed to being oriented around a broader notion of education as a public good.

A student's major simply must mean more than a credential for a first job out of college. I cannot think of a more depressingly low bar for what students should be striving to achieve and experience while they're in college. Rather than worrying about a student's "qualifications," institutions should be focused instead on their preparation for the challenges of life after graduation.

We don't really know what challenges are in front of us, so allowing the trajectory of a student's life to be shaped according to a made-up statistic pushed by people and organizations with agendas that are demonstrably antifreedom sounds like a bad thing. So whatever we do, let's not do that.

CHAPTER 14

The Surveillance-Free Institution

Writing at his personal blog, University of Maryland PhD candidate Jeffrey Moro declares that we should "abolish cop shit" in the classroom. "Cop shit" is shorthand for any tool that enforces student compliance with standards that are often arbitrary and divorced from learning. Standardized tests? Cop shit. Behavior tracking apps like ClassDojo? Total cop shit. Even the five-paragraph essay itself, with its rigid template and an assessment model predicated on adherence to that template, is a form of cop shit.

Moro lists other things he identifies as cop shit at the college level, including ed-tech that tracks our students' every move; plagiarism detection software; needlessly harsh policies about tardiness; assignments that require copying out honor code statements; "rigor," "grit," and "discipline"; and any interface with *actual cops*, such as reporting students' immigration status to ICE.[1]

All of these methods are inconsistent with the goals of fostering student agency and critical thinking. The need for plagiarism detection software such as Turnitin suggests either ineffective and unimaginative pedagogy or unacceptable teaching conditions that burden instructors with too many students to do their work effectively. The other items on Moro's list are either meaningless education buzzwords ("grit," "rigor") or policies that actually stoke antagonism between students and instructors.

As the coronavirus pandemic continues, the early weeks of the 2020 fall semester have seen a significant uptick in universities engaging in cop shit as they attempt to enforce restrictions on public gatherings of students. Threats of suspension and even expulsion have been commonplace, and yet the gatherings continue. The predictable actions of students in these contexts should show us the limits of policies that are rooted in enforced compliance to achieve pedagogical goals. Even if students appear to be performing well, when compliance is at the center of the experience, it is difficult to know if they're learning anything other than how to please authority. Keeping students from gathering and socializing on campus was going to be a heavy lift regardless of the tactics, but experts suggest that with the mix of shame and threats that seem to show up frequently, we're doomed to failure.[2]

Courses held over Zoom or other video conferencing software are causing other tensions involving cop shit. Should students be required to keep their cameras on? Should points be deducted if eyeballs wander or if a distracting pet wanders into view? The discussion often centers around how to enforce compliance, rather than on what sort of policies may be conducive to establishing the best possible atmosphere for distance learning during a pandemic.

Perhaps the worst manifestation of cop shit is remote proctoring software, such as Proctorio and Honorlock, which require students to submit to being spied on as they do their work. Honorlock boasts of technology that prevents students from using multiple devices simultaneously to prevent accessing answers online. It also features the Live Pop-In™, which allows a proctor to spontaneously jump into a view of the student and their work/living space.

If instruction requires literal surveillance to maintain "integrity," we are well past the point of meaningful learning. Authentic pedagogy has been thrown out the window and it's been replaced with a credentialing machine, increasingly monitored by AI.

Leaving cop shit behind and replacing it with a culture of genuine accountability coupled with appropriate remedies (and even punishments) when community standards are breached will be a far more effective strategy. Imagine if students had been invited to collaborate on institutional policy and practices in managing the pandemic. Wouldn't that have given them a fuller sense of ownership over the policies and their success or failure? Might we have seen a different outcome?

It's common nowadays to see students as antagonists to the well-being of a college or university. This point of view is, in every way, ass-backward.

Against Algorithmic Intervention

One manifestation of cop shit on campus is "spy shit," technology which often works in the background to monitor student behavior and then steer students according to algorithmic calculations derived from aggregated data. It is my hope that we will embrace the elimination of this type of technology in educational contexts. It is inconsistent with the principle of freedom implied by a "free" college or university. It's also counterproductive to both student learning and students' ability to develop their own agency.

As we consider the use of aggregated data in higher education contexts, here is the most important truth to keep in mind: *individuals are not averages*. What may be true in the aggregate may not be true for each individual that is part of that aggregate. "Big data" can tell you how many shoppers in total are going to leave the grocery store with potato chips on Memorial Day weekend, but it cannot tell, definitively, if an individual shopper is going to buy potato chips.

Because I believe educational institutions are morally and ethically bound to protect the rights and freedoms of individual students, using aggregated data to control or influence their choices in nontransparent ways is a betrayal of the core mission of higher education and a violation of trust.

Most of the algorithmic interventions campuses currently

utilize are a by-product of the dysfunctional system we are hoping to disrupt with our move toward the sustainable, resilient, and free college or university. In our current system, however, these interventions are more than common—they are heading toward being ubiquitous.

Fortunately, tracking software that attempts to gauge prospective student interest in an institution based on their interactions with the university website will not be necessary when schools are no longer in the fundamental business of enrolling students for tuition dollars.[3] As they're currently employed, these predictive analytics attached to a university's website can help identify wealthier students who are more likely to be able to pay tuition, which results in additional recruiting attention, therefore making them more likely to take a slot in an incoming class.

To the institution, this is a sensible strategy to protect a necessary revenue stream. To the individual student who is less wealthy, and who does not get into the state university closest to her home—which might allow her to save money—this system may have economic effects that quite literally constrain the rest of her life.

For a college or university, location tracking software, which identifies where "successful" students are spending their time and then attempts to "nudge" other students toward similar behaviors, is aimed at improving persistence and retention.[4] At the individual level, however, we may have created a nice little anxiety app, where every alert is an opportunity to dump a little more cortisol into the old system and spend some quality time worrying, rather than, you know, studying (or playing or sleeping).

Even more troubling initiatives are being explored. The "precision education" movement is working on something called "polygenic scores"—a combination of multiple genes that, according to the movement's adherents, correlate with ultimate educational achievement. Their goal is to predict a person's future education outcomes based on their DNA. In their research, the polygenic score accounted for "11 percent of the variation in education across individuals."

What does all this mean at the individual level? Not much. The predictive power of the polygenic score is incredibly weak. Someone scoring in the ninety-eighth percentile for their polygenic score could fall anywhere between the second and ninety-eighth percentile for academic achievement.

Individuals are not averages, and a gussied up, high-tech eugenics is still eugenics.

In each of these cases, we can see a disconnect between the needs of the institution and the needs and rights of the individual. A college must raise its graduation rate, and therefore, nudging particular students toward particular fields of study where the aggregates say they're more likely to persist must be a good thing. But what if it pushes some individuals who could have succeeded on one path onto another that is ultimately lower-paying?[5] Those individuals have been demonstrably harmed by being subject to the "wisdom" of aggregation.

How would we square a low polygenic score for education that may exclude an individual from pursuing postsecondary education at all with our fundamental ideas about basic freedoms?

We wouldn't, because we couldn't.

Kyle Jones, a researcher of information policy and ethics in the Department of Library and Information Science at Indiana University-Purdue University Indianapolis (IUPUI), has identified the fundamental tension of using these sorts of technologies in the operations of colleges and universities:

> Those who advocate for learning analytics have an educational policy agenda in mind. What they choose to quantify and analyze in part signals

> what is important to them. But what is important or
> valuable for those who have the power to pursue
> analytics may not be the same for those who become
> the subjects and targets of learning analytics.[6]

In other words, we cannot in good conscience impose this sort of technology upon students. In a healthy institution focused on teaching and learning, algorithm-derived course "pathways" would have no purpose. They are utterly disconnected from the institutional mission, wholly rooted in institutional "operations." If technologies are going to be utilized at postsecondary institutions, they must be both transparent and controlled by the students themselves.

In a way, the embrace of these technologies is another example of "institutional awe." The underlying conditions of austerity and scarcity are what make these technological interventions potentially attractive. Mississippi State needs to try to enroll as many out-of-state students as possible because they don't receive sufficient funding from the state itself. If sufficient funding was guaranteed, Mississippi State wouldn't have to pay outside consultants to track clicks on the university website and provide reports of prospects' "affinity scores." Individual students likewise wouldn't bear the unnecessary expense of potentially being forced into an out-of-state college because the slots at their home institutions have been taken by wealthy students from other states.

If we remove these inhospitable conditions by embracing the sustainable and resilient framework, both students and the institutions they attend will thrive. This means a maximal embrace of freedom, and a rejection of the principles of scientific management and data tracking that are inconsistent with individual agency.

Individuals are not averages. Treating students as full human beings rather than customers, as people who are fully in charge of their own destinies rather than subjects of administrative and algorithmic control, is the bare minimum of what we should expect from our public colleges and universities.

We must do better. I am hopeful we can.

CONCLUSION

Hopes and Dreams and Other Fine Things

It is a challenge for any book to gain traction in the attention marketplace, and this book will have it harder than others. A big part of this is due to the kinds of higher education stories that tend to capture the broader public's attention. On the same weekend I am writing this conclusion, outside of the various stories about how campuses are dealing with the coronavirus, the top stories in the news about higher education are:

(1) "The Secret of Elite College Admissions"[1] by Jeffrey Selingo in the *Wall Street Journal,* an excerpt from his forthcoming book, *Who Gets in and Why: A Year Inside College Admissions.* The excerpt is a highly compelling look at the sausage-making of the admissions committees at highly selective institutions.

(2) "College Is Everywhere Now" by Taylor Lorenz in the *New York Times.* The subhead to the story is "Yale students in Barbados. Michigan students in Brooklyn. Berkeley students in Las Vegas? Off-campus housing is way off-campus now."[2] There is a section titled "The Summer Camp as Dorm." You can imagine what the bulk of the story is about.

Lorenz is one of the best technology reporters in the country. Selingo has been one of the most-read voices on higher education for over a decade. Both of these stories are about the small minority of students who attend highly selective institutions, many or most of whom come from highly privileged backgrounds.

Don't get me wrong; they are both good stories. They have rocketed around my Twitter feed this weekend for good reason. They are stories that reflect the audiences of the publications in which they appeared. They also reflect the lives of the vast majority of the people who work in high-profile media jobs and for our few remaining legacy publications.

But both stories have very little to do with the day-to-day experiences of the vast majority of students pursuing a postsecondary credential. And yet, for the broader public, those stories will represent what college is as a whole.

The students who would be helped most by tuition-free public higher education are largely invisible to the people who shape the broader cultural narratives that have so much influence on public opinion. One of the most significant tasks ahead is to challenge and change these narratives.

My hope is that this book might be useful to others who share the goal of building tuition-free institutions that will provide access and opportunity to all students who qualify and desire the chance to realize their potential. My hope is that those like me, people who have dedicated their time inside of public higher education institutions to teaching and learning, will recognize their experiences in mine and believe that better days could be ahead. Let this book be a wedge to crack open the conversation and offer some ammunition in the quest for other voices to be heard.

Even if our worst fears about the future of public higher education are realized, at least this book will exist as a testament that there were some people who proposed an alternative.

At the opening of this book, I talked about how hopeful I am because of how clear the vision and possibilities are for the sustainable, resilient, and free public institution of higher education. It requires nothing other than a belief that change is possible and a willingness to act on that belief.

Who will believe with me?

August 30, 2020
Mount Pleasant, South Carolina

APPENDIX

The Chapters I Didn't Write

There is a list of at least a half dozen chapters I wanted to write for this book, along with numerous other threads of discussion and argument that are relevant to the issues raised in the book that I wanted to integrate. But I'm working under both space constraints and a deadline, so they didn't make it into the main text. I'll try to deal with some of them in lightning-round fashion here.

QUESTION: Can states or institutions opt out of receiving additional federal dollars to make their school(s) tuition-free if they'd rather stick with the current system?

ANSWER: Of course. If states feel that they have a more sustainable model hewing more closely to the present status quo, they should pursue that route. I can even imagine that a small handful of elite state flagships (the so-called "public Ivies") could try to compete their way to success. My guess is that these institutions would be very few in number; because being competitive would require increased state investment, even they would benefit from this new framework.

QUESTION: What if the inevitable process of political compromise made it so only the first two years of postsecondary education were tuition-free? Would this still be worth doing?

ANSWER: Absolutely, positively, 100 percent yes. This would mean community colleges, or the first two years of four-year college, would be tuition free, which is not a bad starting point.

QUESTION: What role should sports have in the sustainable, resilient, and free public higher education institution?

ANSWER: It's important to remember that in order to operate, the vast majority of college athletics departments run at a deficit and require subsidies drawn from institutional funds.[1] At the same time, big time football from the Power 5 conferences—the Big 10, Pac-12, SEC, ACC, and the Big 12—and major college basketball are billion-dollar businesses. It is impossible to run these businesses in ways that are consistent with institutions that are run as nonprofits and that are supposed to be dedicated to education and learning. In my view, Power 5 football and major college basketball should be spun into for-profit entities that run independently of educational institutions. Teams will license the logos and trademarks of various schools and pay appropriate rent for the use of campus facilities. These sports will be pure sources of revenue for schools themselves, not liabilities. Players should also be paid. They are participants in professional development leagues that generate billions of dollars in revenue. Some of this pay could come as an education credit, good for a college degree to be earned in six years of consecutive or nonconsecutive study, but this will not be the only source of compensation. Finally, nonrevenue generating sports will be resized to reflect a school's available budget. Some of the revenue drawn from the for-profit athletics entity could and should be used to support these sports, but athletics subsidies that have previously come from student tuition and fees must end. Tuition is for the cost of instruction.

QUESTION: How do we deal with the problem of textbook costs?

ANSWER: Textbook costs, much like adjunctification, are what I call a "slippage problem," where incremental increases that we know are bad—but that aren't bad enough to act decisively on at any given moment—accrue over time until we have an unacceptable situation. Addressing this slippage problem will require a combination of actions, many of which are already in the works. But primarily, faculty must act affirmatively and deliberately to try to limit the cost of textbooks as much as possible.

In 2017, I wrote about how I'd stopped using *Writing Fiction: A Guide to Narrative Craft*, by Janet Burroway, in my creative writing courses because it had simply become too expensive to justify a list price of $113.80 for a 400-page paperback that would sell for a maximum of $18.95 if it had been anything other than a textbook.[2]

Burroway was also bothered by the cost of her own book, so when a window to regain the rights opened, she took them and sought out a new publisher, the University of Chicago Press, that agreed to keep costs down. The book now retails for $22.50.

This kind of deliberate act is necessary on a mass scale and can be enacted simply by faculty being mindful of choosing texts and materials that are the least-costly, acceptable student resources.

QUESTION: Are grades "cop shit?"

ANSWER: Pretty much. Traditional grading systems, as they're often used, are primarily tools of compliance that work against student engagement and the development of agency. Personally, getting rid of traditional grading was crucial in increasing the rigor of my own classes.

For anyone who's curious about alternatives to traditional grading, I recommend *Ungrading: Why Rating Students Undermines Learning (and What to Do Instead)*, edited by

Susan D. Blum, which includes a chapter by yours truly on how Wile E. Coyote is the hero of "ungrading."[3]

QUESTION: Won't students be less serious about their education if they don't have to pay?

ANSWER: I hear this question a lot and honestly do not understand it. Do full-scholarship students take their educations less seriously when they don't have to pay? Do wealthy children take their educations less seriously because their parents are paying? Some do, some don't.

The opportunity to accrue the benefits of an education is all a student needs for proper motivation. Those students who do not take it seriously will be excused from the institution, a mechanism that has always been in place.

QUESTION: Won't institutions be overwhelmed with students if postsecondary education is tuition-free?

ANSWER: We can expect an increase in those pursuing a postsecondary credential, but it is important to note that while I primarily focus on colleges and universities in this book, other postsecondary credentials should also be supported by public funds, provided those credentials come from nonprofit, public entities.

States will be able to manage their ecosystems according to need and demand. If more slots are needed at selective institutions, they can scale up there. If the open-access institutions see an increase in demand, they can scale up there. It's also important to remember that the pursuit of the credential is only open to those who qualify. If more students are qualified, that strikes me as an unalloyed good. It means more people are being educated.

QUESTION: Are you really abandoning all private colleges and universities?

ANSWER: As I mentioned earlier, private nonprofit institutions that are aligned with the mission of enrolling students from lower socioeconomic tiers and improving the lifetime outcomes of those students deserve continued support. This is one of the things that must be considered as the specifics of these policies are put into place. We should pay particular attention to helping HBCUs (some of which are private), which have suffered longstanding neglect while also occupying a unique and vital role in the higher education ecosystem.

However, when it comes to the wealthy elite institutions that dominate the discourse but educate very few students (who are primarily drawn from the already wealthy) my preference is they cease to benefit from public subsidy. They'll be fine.

QUESTION: Aren't we going to lose some institutions no matter what?

ANSWER: Almost certainly. The scope of the recession brought on by the pandemic will make it very difficult to save every existing institution, some of which were already threatened prior to the outbreak of the coronavirus. Small private colleges without big endowments will be especially vulnerable. States with lower populations of college-seeking students may also potentially see a reduction in the number of schools in their system.

For public institutions, it is important that the discussion revolve around the needs and the health of the overall ecosystem, rather than the exigencies of budgets. Making institutions tuition-free should make this easier.

QUESTION: Do you think there's any chance any of this is actually going to happen?

ANSWER: As I say, in many ways I'm hopeful, but the problems of the political economy stand in the way. There is much work to be done on many different fronts, and we can expect turmoil and division in the foreseeable future, which may make it even more difficult to come together to solve big problems.

In reality, making college tuition-free would provide a macroeconomic boost over time. It would support the communities in which colleges exist and play a role in reducing our historically high levels of inequality. Making public colleges and universities tuition-free would positively impact every state in the union, which may make it easier to find common ground on the issue.

But by itself, tuition-free college isn't a panacea. The good news is that if it does happen, it's likely that we're also tackling other big problems, and we've turned a corner on a new age where we as a society once again believe it's possible to act for the common good.

NOTES

Preface

[1] Marken, Stephanie. "Half in U.S. Now Consider College Education Very Important," *Gallup,* December 30, 2019. https://www.gallup.com/education/272228/half-consider-college-education-important.aspx.

[2] Fletcher, Michael A. "White High School Dropouts Are Wealthier than Black and Hispanic College Graduates. Can a New Policy Tool Fix That?" *The Washington Post.* March 10, 2015. https://www.washingtonpost.com/news/wonk/wp/2015/03/10/white-high-school-dropouts-are-wealthier-than-black-and-hispanic-college-graduates-can-a-new-policy-tool-fix-that/.

[3] "What's the Average GPA for Medical School Matriculants?" *Kaplan.* https://www.kaptest.com/study/mcat/whats-the-average-gpa-for-medical-school-matriculants/.

[4] Kowarski, Ilana. "What Is a Good College GPA in J.D. Admissions?" *US News and World Report*, August 21, 2018. https://www.usnews.com/education/best-graduate-schools/top-law-schools/articles/2018-08-21/how-high-is-the-typical-college-gpa-among-accepted-law-school-applicants.

[5] Younghans, Johanna. "One in Five College Students Reported Thoughts of Suicide in Last Year," *Assocation of American Universities*, September 10, 2018. https://www.aau.edu/research-scholarship/featured-research-topics/one-five-college-students-reported-thoughts-suicide.

[6] Vega, Lilia. "The History of UC Tuition Since 1868," *The Daily Californian,* December 22, 2014. https://www.dailycal.org/2014/12/22/history-uc-tuition-since-1868/.

[7] "Tuition and Cost of Attendance," *University of California.* https://admission.universityofcalifornia.edu/tuition-financial-aid/tuition-cost-of-attendance/.

[8] In 1985, the minimum wage in California was $3.35 an hour.

[9] Danz, Jack. "Hope Center Releases Report on Student Basic Needs Insecurity during COVID-19," *The Temple News,* June 18, 2020. https://temple-news.com/hope-center-releases-report-on-student-basic-needs-insecurity-during-covid-19/.

Chapter 1

[1] Leachman, Michael. "New CBO Projections Suggest Even Bigger State Shortfalls." *Center on Budget and Policy Priorities*, April 29, 2020. https://www.cbpp.org/blog/new-cbo-projections-suggest-even-bigger-state-shortfalls.

[2] Toppo, Greg. "Partial, and Uneven, Recovery from Recession," *Inside Higher Ed*, April 9, 2019. https://www.insidehighered.com/news/2019/04/09/student-public-spending-recovers-halfway-recession-study.

[3] "State Funding Remains below Historic Levels as Public Colleges Brace for a Recession and Expected Budget Cuts," *State Higher Education Finance,* 2020. https://sheeomain.wpengine.com/project/state-higher-education-finance/.

[4] Pan, Deanna. "College of Charleston's Shortfall Rises to $2.1 Million," *The Post and Courier*, December 2, 2015. https://www.postandcourier.com/archives/college-of-charleston-s-shortfall-rises-to-million/article_af7cb96d-380e-510f-a85a-9b2d1e9f8fe0.html.

[5] McLean, Danielle. "With Latest Layoffs, U. of Akron Has Lost Almost a Quarter of Its Faculty Since Pandemic Began," *The Chronicle of Higher Education*, July 15, 2020. https://www.chronicle.com/article/With-Latest-Layoffs-U-of/249186.

[6] "Economic Diversity and Student Outcomes at America's Colleges and Universities: Find Your College," *The New York Times*. https://www.nytimes.com/interactive/projects/college-mobility/.

[7] Newfield, Christopher. *The Great Mistake: How We Wrecked Public Universities and How We Can Fix Them*. Baltimore: Johns Hopkins University Press, 2016.

Chapter 2

[1] Walsh, James D. "The Coming Disruption," *New York,* May 11, 2020. https://nymag.com/intelligencer/2020/05/scott-galloway-future-of-college.html.

[2] Gershgorn, Dave. "Former Google CEO Wants to Create a Government-Funded University to Train A.I. Coders," *OneZero*, July 21, 2020. https://onezero.medium.com/former-google-ceo-wants-to-create-a-government-funded-university-to-train-a-i-coders-9a2df09c5bce.

[3] Don't hate. I was a twenty-year-old dude.

[4] US Department of Education. "Debt Burden: A Comparison of 1992–93 and 1999–2000 Bachelor's Degree Recipients a Year after Graduating," *National Center for Education Statistics*, March 2005. https://nces.ed.gov/pubs2005/2005170.pdf.

[5] This may already have been achieved. Certainly, companies like Facebook and Google seem to exist beyond the reach of government regulation.

[6] To see what this looks like when coupled with climate collapse, check out Margaret Atwood's *MaddAddam* trilogy.

Chapter 3

[1] "Fixing a Hole: Berkeley Seeks to Repair Its Budget," *Berkeley News,* November 16, 2016. https://news.berkeley.edu/2016/11/16/budget-qa-carol-christ/.

[2] It is worth noting that the vast majority of community colleges, as well as schools in the California state system, schools which are not beholden to prestige, committed very early on to a primarily online fall 2020 semester.

[3] Pompeo, Joe. "The Hedge Fund Vampire That Bleeds Newspapers Dry Now has the *Chicago Tribune* by the Throat," *Vanity Fair*, February 5, 2020. https://www.vanityfair.com/news/2020/02/hedge-fund-vampire-alden-global-capital-that-bleeds-newspapers-dry-has-chicago-tribune-by-the-throat.

[4] Murphy, Dermot. "When Local Papers Close, Costs Rise for Local Governments," *Columbia Journalism Review*, June 27, 2020. https://www.cjr.org/united_states_project/public-finance-local-news.php.

[5] Anderson, Meg. "Amid Pandemic, Hospitals Lay Off 1.4M Workers in April," *NPR,* May 10, 2020. https://www.npr.org/2020/05/10/853524764/amid-pandemic-hospitals-lay-off-1-4m-workers-in-april.

[6] Arnsdorf, Isaac. "How Rich Investors, Not Doctors, Profit from Marking Up ER Bills," *ProPublica*, June 12, 2020. https://www.propublica.org/article/how-rich-investors-not-doctors-profit-from-marking-up-er-bills/amp?.

[7] Orszag, Peter R. "Why Public Universities Are Getting Shortchanged," *Bloomberg*, October 17, 2018. https://www.bloomberg.com/opinion/articles/2018-10-17/health-care-costs-push-states-to-cut-funding-for-universities.

[8] The curious can see how and why the push toward competition has tragically distorted the way we teach writing in my 2018 book, *Why They Can't Write: Killing the Five-Paragraph Essay and Other Necessities*, Johns Hopkins University Press, 2019.

Chapter 4

[1] University of Michigan. "General Fund Budget Snapshot," 2020. https://publicaffairs.vpcomm.umich.edu/key-issues/tuition/general-fund-budget-tutorial/.

[2] Mitchell, Michael, et al. "A Lost Decade in Higher Education Funding," *Center on Budget and Policy Priorities*, August 23, 2017. https://www.cbpp.org/research/state-budget-and-tax/a-lost-decade-in-higher-education-funding.

[3] Whitford, Emma. "Public Higher Ed Funding Still Has Not Recovered from 2008 Recession," *Inside Higher Ed*, May 5, 2020. https://www.insidehighered.com/news/2020/05/05/public-higher-education-worse-spot-ever-heading-recession.

[4] Shout-out to my fellow aficionados of *The Wire*.

[5] Lederman, Doug. "'Manipulating,' Er, Influencing *U.S. News*," *Inside Higher Ed*, June 3, 2009. https://www.insidehighered.com/news/2009/06/03/manipulating-er-influencing-us-news.

[6] Slotnik, Daniel E. and Pérez-Peña, Richard. "College Says It Exaggerated SAT Figures for Ratings," *The New York Times,* June 30, 2012. https://www.nytimes.com/2012/01/31/education/claremont-mckenna-college-says-it-exaggerated-sat-figures.html?smid=pl-share.

[7] Burd, Stephen. "Undermining Pell: Volume IV," *New America*, October 29, 2018. https://www.insidehighered.com/sites/default/server_files/media/UNDERMINING_PELL_VOLUME_IV_2018-10-29_134242.pdf.

[8] Belkin, Douglas. "College Financial-Aid Loophole: Wealthy Parents Transfer Guardianship of Their Teens to Get Aid," *The Wall Street Journal*, July 29, 2019. https://www.wsj.com/articles/college-financial-aid-loophole-wealthy-parents-transfer-guardianship-of-their-teens-to-get-aid-11564450828.

Chapter 5

[1] Ray, Julie and Marken, Stephanie. "Life in College Matters for Life after College," *Gallup*, May 6, 2014. https://news.gallup.com/poll/168848/life-college-matters-life-college.aspx.

[2] Huang, Sandra Liu. "Education Unlocks Opportunity and Agency That Can Change the Trajectory of a Family for Generations," *Chan Zuckberg Initiative*. https://chanzuckerberg.com/education/.

[3] Tough, Paul. "Her School Offered a Path to the Middle Class. Will COVID-19 Block It?" *The New York Times Magazine*, September 15, 2020. https://www.nytimes.com/interactive/2020/09/09/magazine/high-school-seniors.html.

[4] Weissmann, Jordan. "43 Percent of White Students Harvard Admits Are Legacies, Jocks or the Kids of Donors and Faculty," *Slate,* September 23, 2019. https://slate.com/business/2019/09/harvard-admissions-affirmative-action-white-students-legacy-athletes-donors.html.

[5] Desai, Saahil. "College Sports Are Affirmative Action for Rich White Students," *The Atlantic*, October 23, 2018. https://www.theatlantic.com/education/archive/2018/10/college-sports-benefits-white-students/573688/.

[6] NCAA. "Play Division III Sports." http://www.ncaa.org/student-athletes/play-division-iii-sports.

[7] Nichols, Andrew Howard. "Segregation Forever?" *The Education Trust*, July 21, 2020. https://edtrust.org/resource/segregation-forever/.

[8] Klor de Alva, Jorge and Schneider, Mark. "Rich Schools, Poor Students: Tapping Large University Endowments to Improve Student Outcomes," *Nexus Research and Policy Center*, April 2015. http://nexusresearch.org/wp-content/uploads/2015/11/Rich-Schools-Poor-Students-Revised-November-2015.pdf. Though, the tax on endowments is now changing.

Chapter 6

[1] Woodhouse, Kellie. "Lazy Rivers and Student Debt," *Inside Higher Ed*, June 15, 2015. https://www.insidehighered.com/news/2015/06/15/are-lazy-rivers-and-climbing-walls-driving-cost-college.

[2] I did my graduate training at McNeese St. University in Lake Charles, Louisiana. The first time I experienced the sensation of breathing the ultra-hot, ultra-humid air, it felt like my face had been smothered with a wet wool blanket and I'd been shoved into a car trunk. It seemed incompatible with life.

[3] Brundrett, Rick. "Tuition, Fees Used to Pay Off Skyrocketing University IOUs," *The Berkeley Independent*, August 20, 2020. https://www.postandcourier.com/berkeley-independent/archives/tuition-fees-used-to-pay-off-skyrocketing-university-ious/article_4a4b0032-4a74-5e31-be94-40b43a13cb27.html.

[4] Selingo, Jeffrey. "Undergraduate Education is Broken. Solutions Start with Faculty and Rigor," *The Washington Post*, June 26, 2017. https://www.washingtonpost.com/news/grade-point/wp/2017/06/26/undergraduate-education-is-broken-solutions-start-with-faculty-and-rigor/.

[5] Haswell, Richard H. "Methodologically Adrift," *College Composition and Communication* (63.3), Feburary 2012. https://secure.ncte. org/library/NCTEFiles/Resources/Journals/CCC/0633-feb2012/ CCC0633Reviews.pdf.

[6] Lederman, Doug. "Less Academically Adrift?" *Inside Higher Ed*, May 20, 2013. https://www.insidehighered.com/news/2013/05/20/ studies-challenge-findings-academically-adrift.

[7] Carey, Kevin. *The End of College: Creating the Future of Learning and the University of Everywhere.* New York: Penguin, 2016.

[8] Young, Jeffrey R. "The New Rock-Star Professor," *Slate*, November 6, 2013. https://slate.com/technology/2013/11/udacity-coursera-should-celebrities-teach-moocs.html.

[9] Rivard, Ry. "Udacity Project on 'Pause,'" *Inside Higher Ed*, July 18, 2013. https://www.insidehighered.com/news/2013/07/18/citing-disappointing-student-outcomes-san-jose-state-pauses-work-udacity.

[10] Chafkin, Max. "Udacity's Sebastian Thrun, Godfather of Free Online Education, Changes Course," *Fast Company*, November 14, 2013. https:// www.fastcompany.com/3021473/udacity-sebastian-thrun- uphill-climb.

[11] Hess, Rick. "A Confession and a Question on Personalized Learning," *Education Week*, February 12, 2018. https://blogs.edweek.org/edweek/ rick_hess_straight_up/2018/02/.a_confession_and_a_question_on_ personalized_learning.html

[12] Watters, Audrey and Goldrick-Rab, Sara. "Techno Fantasies," *Inside Higher Ed*. March 26, 2015. https://www.insidehighered.com/ views/2015/03/26/essay-challenging-kevin-careys-new-book-higher-education.

[13] Carey, Kevin. "The 'Public' in Public College Could be Endangered," *The New York Times*, May 5, 2020. https://www.nytimes. com/2020/05/05/ upshot/public-colleges-endangered-pandemic.html.

Chapter 7

[1] Editorial Board. "We All Saw This Coming," *The Daily Tar Heel*, August 16, 2020. https://www.dailytarheel.com/article/2020/08/covid-clusters-edit-0816.

[2] Burke, Lilah. "Early Adopters," *Inside Higher Ed,* August 21, 2020. https://www.insidehighered.com/news/2020/08/21/early-movers-online-fall-dont-regret-decision.

[3] Cottom, Tressie McMillan. Twitter post. September 5, 2020, 11:40 a.m. https://twitter.com/tressiemcphd/status/1302270462865670144

[4] Stone, Michael. "What Happened When American States Tried Providing Tuition-Free College," *Time*, April 4, 2016. https://time.com/4276222/free-college/. There were nominal "fees" prior to that date, but they were truly nominal.

[5] Sherwin, Amanda. "Could CUNY Be Tuition-Free Again? *Gotham Gazette,* July 20, 2016. https://www.gothamgazette.com/city/6444-could-cuny-be-tuition-free-again.

[6] Him again!

[7] "Tennessee Promise Annual Report," 2019. https://issuu.com/thec-tsac/docs/tn_promise_report_2019_final.

[8] It's worth noting that one of the chief culprits of ever-increasing costs is the cost of providing health care benefits to employees.

[9] Deming, David. "Tuition-Free College Could Cost Less Than You Think," *The New York Times*, July 19, 2019. https://www.nytimes.com/2019/07/19/business/tuition-free-college.html.

[10] Congressional Budget Office. "Distribution of Federal Support for Students Pursuing Higher Education in 2016," 2018. https://www.cbo.gov/system/files/2018-06/53732-taxexpenditureshighereducation.pdf.

[11] Newfield, Christopher. "Only Free College Can Save Us from This Crisis," *The Chronicle of Higher Education*, April 9, 2020. https://www.chronicle.com/article/only-free-college-can-save-us-from-this-crisis/.

[12] Fullwiler Scott, et al. "The Macroeconomic Effects of Student Debt Cancellation," Levy Economics Institute, February 2018. http://www.levyinstitute.org/pubs/rpr_2_6.pdf.

[13] Note that this also was done during a period of low unemployment.

[14] Miller, Claire Cain. "Americans Are Having Fewer Babies. They Told Us Why," *The New York Times*, July 5, 2018. https://www.nytimes.com/2018/07/05/upshot/americans-are-having-fewer-babies-they-told-us-why.html.

[15] Steinbaum, Marshall. "Is Student Debt Cancellation Regressive? No," *Current Affairs*, June 15, 2019. https://www.currentaffairs.org/2019/06/is-student-debt-cancellation-regressive-no.

Chapter 8
[1] Ettarh, Fobazi. "Vocational Awe and Librarianship: The Lies We Tell Ourselves," *In the Library with the Lead Pipe*, January 10, 2018. http://www.inthelibrarywiththeleadpipe.org/2018/vocational-awe/.

[2] Guskiewicz, Kevin. "Message from Chancellor Guskiewicz on Letter from the Orange County Health Department." https://www.unc.edu/posts/2020/08/05/message-from-guskiewicz-on-letter-from-the-orange-county-health-department/.

[3] Bauer-Wolf, Jeremy. "Why UNC's Plan to Reopen Its Flagship Campus Unraveled So Fast," *Education Dive*, August 19, 2020. https://www.educationdive.com/news/why-uncs-plan-to-reopen-its-flagship-campus-unraveled-so-fast/583821/.

[4] Murphy, Kate. "Campus Workers Sue UNC System, Claiming Unsafe Working Conditions During Pandemic," *The News & Observer*, August 10, 2020. https://www.newsobserver.com/news/local/education/article244858712.html.

[5] Obviously, this would have to be done in a nonpartisan way.

Chapter 9
[1] Flaherty, Colleen. "A Non-Tenure-Track Profession?" *Inside Higher Ed*, October 12, 2018. https://www.insidehighered.com/news/2018/10/12/about-three-quarters-all-faculty-positions-are-tenure-track-according-new-aaup.

[2] The University of Illinois at Urbana-Champaign, Virginia Tech, and Clemson.

[3] At most. Some had course releases that took them below this threshold.

[4] I sometimes think about the money I did not earn because I was not an assistant professor in those years (around $300k), but then I must stop thinking about it because it still makes me upset.

[5] Schwartz, Charles. "Disaggregating the Costs of Academic Missions at the University of California," October 22, 2016. https://www.ocf.berkeley.edu/~schwrtz/DCAM16.pdf.

[6] The exception is, of course, sponsored research, paid for with outside funding and grants. Work classified as "departmental research" does not fall under this category.

[7] In most departments, the number of contingent faculty outnumbers tenured faculty, but I want to keep the math easy for purposes of this illustration. For a spreadsheet that allows for data entry of every member of a department in order to calculate the specific teaching labor wage gap, you can go here: https://docs.google.com/spreadsheets/d/1hPvw1Z6D_nkIqA12JC1tPAHLTabGmVq5yrw10DoOTD0/edit?usp=sharing.

Chapter 10
[1] June, Audrey Williams. "Frustrated Faculty Struggle to Defend Tenure before It's Too Late" *The Chronicle of Higher Education*, June 17, 2018. https://www.chronicle.com/article/frustrated-faculty-struggle-to-defend-tenure-before-its-too-late/.

[2] This would entail creating different paths to tenure for positions with different roles inside the institution. "Teaching tenure" would have to become a more widespread practice.

[3] Part-time positions should be limited to adjunct faculty who fit the traditional definition of a professional outside the institution offering that expertise to the institution.

[4] While making sure all stakeholders in the institution actually have a share of that governance.

[5] "College Students Are More Diverse Than Ever. Faculty and Administrators Are Not," *AAC&U News*, March 2019. https://www.aacu.org/aacu-news/newsletter/2019/march/facts-figures.

[6] Flaherty, Colleen. "Professors Still More Likely Than Students to Be White." *Inside Higher Ed,* August 1, 2019. https://www.insidehighered.com/quicktakes/2019/08/01/professors-still-more-likely-students-be-white.

[7] Dozens, maybe even hundreds of TV and film comedy writers have been published at *McSweeney's* online over the years, including the current head writer for the *Daily Show* and the show runner for *Last Week Tonight with John Oliver*.

[8] I believed in timely responses, but occasionally I would hold back from responding to submissions from certain contributors knowing that they were going to boomerang a new piece right back to my inbox.

[9] My successor in 2008, Chris Monks, took what I'd started and moved it significantly forward. The site is now considerably more diverse in terms of contributors and content in all ways.

[10] Harris, Paul C. "Letter to Provost," March 9, 2020. https://drive.google.com/file/d/16KKaKGkTYJwBHFCoJiHUobu88ruyZVZG/view.

[11] Harris, Taylor. "Whiteness Can't Save Us," *Catapult*, June 10, 2020. https://catapult.co/stories/taylor-harris-on-police-violence-racism-church-parenting-black-kids.

[12] Flaherty, Colleen. "UVA Reverses Tenure Denial," *Inside Higher Ed*, July 27, 2020. https://www.insidehighered.com/quicktakes/2020/07/27/uva-reverses-tenure-denial

Chapter 11

[1] "Pew Research Center surveys of U.S. adults conducted by telephone July 10–15, 2019, June 8–18, 2017, Sept. 16–Oct 4, 2015, and Feb. 8–12, 2012." Pew Research Center, Washington, DC (August 19, 2019). https://www.pewsocialtrends.org/essay/the-growing-partisan-divide-in-views-of-higher-education/.

[2] Vasquez, Michael. "As Turning Point USA Grows, So Does Charlie Kirk's Salary," *The Chronicle of Higher Education*, July 10, 2020. https://www.chronicle.com/article/as-turning-point-usa-grows-so-does-charlie-kirks-salary.

[3] Shulevitz, Judith. "In College and Hiding from Scary Ideas," *The New York Times,* March 21, 2015. https://www.nytimes.com/2015/03/22/opinion/sunday/judith-shulevitz-hiding-from-scary-ideas.html.

[4] Friedersdorf, Conor. "A Food Fight at Oberlin College," *The Atlantic*, December 21, 2015. https://www.theatlantic.com/politics/archive/2015/12/the-food-fight-at-oberlin-college/421401/.

[5] Hartocollis, Anemona. "Yale Professor and Wife, Targets of Protests, Resign as College Heads," *The New York Times*. May 26, 2016. https://www.nytimes.com/2016/05/27/us/yale-professor-and-wife-targets-of-protests-resign-as-college-heads.html.

[6] Lukianoff, Greg and Haidt, Jonathan. "The Coddling of the American Mind," *The Atlantic*, September 2015. https://www.theatlantic.com/magazine/archive/2015/09/the-coddling-of-the-american-mind/399356/.

[7] McMurtrie, Beth. "A 'Devastating Account' of Diversity at Yale," *The Chronicle of Higher Education*, May 25, 2016. https://www.chronicle.com/article/a-devastating-account-of-diversity-at-yale/?cid2=gen_login_refresh&cid=gen_sign_in.

[8] Nelson, Libby. "Yale's Big Fight over Sensitivity and Free Speech, Explained," *Vox,* November 7, 2015. https://www.vox.com/2015/11/7/9689330/yale-halloween-email.

[9] Well, at least it did until Donald Trump came along. The demonization of college students engaging in protests in which their causes are undeniably righteous has helped pave the way for such antidemocratic movements.

[10] Hopefully, some readers knew that something was up with the reference to the 200th anniversary of the Bill of Rights.

[11] Friedersdorf, Conor. "The New Intolerance of Student Activism," *The Atlantic*, November 9, 2015. https://www.theatlantic.com/politics/

archive/2015/11/the-new-intolerance-of-student-activism-at-yale/414810/.

[12] Campbell, Colin and Horowitz, Jonathan. "Does College Influence Sociopolitical Attitudes?" *Sociology of Education* 89, no. 1 (January 2016): 40–58. https://journals.sagepub.com/doi/abs/10.1177/0038040715617224.

[13] Mariani, Mack D. and Hewitt, Gordon J. "Indoctrination U.? Faculty Ideology and Changes in Student Political Orientation." *PS: Political Science & Politics* 41, no. 4 (2008): 773–83. https://www.cambridge.org/core/journals/ps-political-science-and-politics/article/indoctrination-u-faculty-ideology-and-changes-in-student-political-orientation/25ABD9B1A3577F27B5659941CD52D6C9.

[14] Mendelberg, Tali, et al. "College Socialization and the Economic Views of Affluent Americans," *American Journal of Political Science,* 61, Issue 3 (2017) 606–623. https://onlinelibrary.wiley.com/doi/abs/10.1111/ajps.12265.

[15] I recommend this excellent overview from Jeffrey Sachs, an academic who studies this phenomenon: Sachs, Jeffrey. "No, Professors Are Not Brainwashing Their Students," *Arc Digital,* Feburary 3, 2020. https://arcdigital.media/no-professors-are-not-brainwashing-their-students-d4694522f413.

[16] Jaschik, Scott. "Professors and Politics: What the Research Says," *Inside Higher Ed*, February 27, 2017. https://www.insidehighered.com/news/2017/02/27/research-confirms-professors-lean-left-questions-assumptions-about-what-means.

[17] Barshay, Jill. "Calculating Faculty Bias against Conservative Students," *The Hechinger Report*, June 24, 2019. https://hechingerreport.org/calculating-faculty-bias-against-conservative-students/.

[18] Abrams, Samuel J. "Swimming against the Current," *Inside Higher Ed*, January 9, 2017. https://www.insidehighered.com/views/2017/01/09/conservatives-are-actually-quite-happy-academe-essay.

[19] PenAmerica. "Campus Free Speech Guide." https://campusfreespeechguide.pen.org/role/faculty/#academic-freedom.

Chapter 12

[1] The "screen time" theory was unconvincing even at the time of the book's publication and is thoroughly debunked now. To the authors' credit, they have acknowledged this in subsequent online updates. See Lukianoff, Greg, et al. "Catching Up with Coddling Part Two: Trigger Warnings, Screen Time v. Social Media, COVID-19 and the Continuing Decline of Generation Z's Mental Health." *The Fire*, May 12, 2020. https://www.thefire.org/catching-up-with-coddling-part-two-trigger-warnings-screen-time-v-social-media-covid-19-and-the-continuing-decline-of-gen-zs-mental-health/.

[2] Children of the sixties were on drugs. My generation—Generation X—had a character defect (slackerdom), but millennials and now Gen Z are actually portrayed as being mentally defective through faults of their own.

[3] Stephens, Bret. "Leave Your Safe Spaces: The 2017 Commencement Address at Hampden-Sydney College," *The New York Times*, May 15, 2017. https://www.nytimes.com/2017/05/15/opinion/leave-your-safe-spaces-the-2017-commencement-address-at-hampden-sydney-college.html?searchResultPosition=1.

[4] Karpf, Dave. Twitter post. August 26, 2020, 5:07 p.m. https://twitter.com/davekarpf/status/1166094950024515584.

[5] Karpf, David. "Bret Stephens Compared Me to a Nazi Propagandist in the New York Times. It Proved My Point," *Esquire*, September 3, 2019. https://www.esquire.com/news-politics/a28892307/david-karpf-bret-stephens-bedbug-nyt-column-response/.

[6] Feinberg, Ashley. "Bret Stephens Backs Out of Bedbug Debate," *Slate*, October 10, 2019. https://slate.com/news-and-politics/2019/10/bret-stephens-backs-out-of-bedbug-debate.html.

[7] In reality, young people would have a solid charge of "complacency" against people of mine, Haidt's, and Lukianoff's generation.

[8] Doucette, T. Greg. Twitter post. May 30, 2020, 11:21 a.m. https://twitter.com/greg_doucette/status/1266751520055459847.

[9] American College Health Association. "National College Health

Assessment," Spring 2018. https://www.acha.org/documents/ncha/
NCHA-II_Spring_2018_Reference_Group_Executive_Summary.pdf.

[10] Horowitz, Juliana Menasce and Graf, Nikki. "Most U.S. Teens See
Anxiety and Depression as a Major Problem among Their Peers," *Pew
Research Center*, Feburary 20, 2019. https://www.pewsocialtrends.
org/2019/02/20/most-u-s-teens-see-anxiety-and-depression-as-a-major-
problem-among-their-peers/.

[11] Belli, Brita. "National Survey: Students' Feelings about High School
Are Mostly Negative," *Yale News*, January 30, 2020. https://news.yale.
edu/2020/01/30/national-survey-students-feelings-about-high-school-
are-mostly-negative.

[12] Robinson, Jennifer. "Academic Ranking May Motivate Some Students,
Alienate Others," *Gallup*, August 9, 2018. https://www.gallup.com/
education/239168/academic-ranking-may-motivate-students-alienate-
others.aspx.

Chapter 13

[1] There are a few exceptions to this that apply much more to community
colleges, which are better positioned to spin up particular programs when
there are specific shortages in specific localities, and then wind them
down if they are no longer necessary. I'm thinking programs in contact
tracing may be a need at this time.

[2] Reed, Matt. "In Defense of English Majors (and Every Other Kind),"
Inside Higher Ed, December 2, 2019. https://www.insidehighered.com/
blogs/confessions-community-college-dean/defense-english-majors-
and-every-other-kind.

[3] Postsecondary Value Commission. https://www.postsecondaryvalue.org.

[4] Bleemer, Zachary. "Wage-by-Major Statistics: Transparency to What
End?" *Inside Higher Ed*, June 24, 2019. https://www.insidehighered.com/
blogs/just-visiting/guest-post-wage-major-statistics-transparency-what-end.

[5] Deming, David. "In the Salary Race, Engineers Sprint but English
Majors Endure," *The New York Times*, October 1, 2019. https://www.
nytimes.com/2019/09/20/business/liberal-arts-stem-salaries.html.

[6] https://www.aacu.org/leap.

[7] https://gened.as.virginia.edu.

[8] Hanstedt, Paul. "But I Like My Third Eye! Or: How I Came to Stop Worrying and Love WAC," *Inside Higher Ed*, January 9, 2019. https://www.insidehighered.com/blogs/just-visiting/guest-blog-i-my-third-eye.

[9] Niemtus, Zofia. "How Do Universities Prepare Graduates for Jobs That Don't Yet Exist?" *The Guardian,* December 20, 2018. https://www.theguardian.com/education/2018/dec/20/how-do-universities-prepare-for-jobs-that-dont-yet-exist.

[10] World Economic Forum. "The Future of Jobs." https://reports.weforum.org/future-of-jobs-2016/chapter-1-the-future-of-jobs-and-skills/.

Chapter 14

[1] Moro, Jeffrey. "Against Cop Shit," https://jeffreymoro.com/blog/2020-02-13-against-cop-shit/.

[2] St. Amour, Madeline. "Will Shame Make Students Stop Partying?" *Inside Higher Ed*, August 21, 2020. https://www.insidehighered.com/news/2020/08/21/colleges-point-fingers-students-partying-spreading-covid-19.

[3] Yes, this technology exists: MacMillan, Douglas and Anderson, Nick. "Student Tracking, Secret Scores: How College Admissions Offices Rank Prospects Before They Apply," *The Washington Post*, October 14, 2019. https://www.washingtonpost.com/business/2019/10/14/colleges-quietly-rank-prospective-students-based-their-personal-data/.

[4] Gardner, Lee. "Students Under Surveillance?" *The Chronicle of Higher Education,* October 13, 2019. https://www.chronicle.com/article/students-under-surveillance/.

[5] Bashay, Jill and Aslanian, Sasha. "Colleges Are Using Big Data to Track Students in an Effort to Boost Graduation Rates, but It Comes at a Cost," *The Hechinger Report*, August 6, 2019. https://hechingerreport.org/predictive-analytics-boosting-college-graduation-rates-also-invade-privacy-and-reinforce-racial-inequities/.

[6] https://www.projectinfolit.org/kyle-jones-smart-talk.html.

Conclusion

[1] Selingo, Jeffrey. "The Secrets of Elite College Admissions," *The Wall Street Journal.* August 28, 2020. https://www.wsj.com/articles/the-secrets-of-elite-college-admissions-11598626784.

[2] Lorenz, Taylor. "College is Everywhere Now," *The New York Times.* August 28, 2020. https://www.nytimes.com/2020/08/28/style/college-collab-houses-coronavirus.html.

Appendix

[1] Wolverton, Brad et al. "The $10 Billion Sports Tab," *The Chronicle of Higher Education.* November 15, 2015. https://www.chronicle.com/article/the-10-billion-sports-tab/.

[2] Warner, John. "Slippage Problems, a Textbook Example," *Inside Higher Ed*, January 16, 2017. https://www.insidehighered.com/blogs/just-visiting/slippage-problems-textbook-example.

[3] https://wvupressonline.com/node/844.

ACKNOWLEDGMENTS

Every book takes a village to come to fruition and this one is no exception.

Thanks to Doug Lederman and Scott Jaschik at *Inside Higher Ed* for providing an outlet that has allowed me to do the thinking required for writing a book without the pain of declaring that I was writing a book.

Thanks to everyone at Belt for bringing this book into the world so quickly and with such care. Thanks to Anne Trubek for understanding what I wanted to do and steering the project in the right direction out of the gate. Thanks to Martha Bayne for taking a draft and clearly making it better. Thanks to Michael Jauchen for fixing and tightening the manuscript in ways I am not capable of doing myself. Thanks to David Wilson for a cover that speaks so strongly.

Thanks to the community of academics, scholars, and instructors who have provided both inspiration and guidance along the way. There are too many to name, but I hope you know who you are.

Thanks to my loved ones for tolerating me when I was in the throes of pulling this project together. I promise this is the last one, at least until the next one.

ABOUT THE AUTHOR

John Warner is a writer, editor, speaker, and consultant with twenty years of college teaching experience at five different colleges and universities. He has been a contributor to *Inside Higher Ed* since 2012, and he writes a weekly column on books and reading for the *Chicago Tribune*.

His book *Why They Can't Write: Killing the Five-Paragraph Essay and Other Necessities* (Johns Hopkins University Press, 2018) challenges the dominant approach to teaching writing as rooted in assessment and standardization. Its companion volume, *The Writer's Practice: Building Confidence in Your Nonfiction Writing* (Penguin, 2019), is an alternative which centers student agency and curiosity as the heart of the writing process. *The Writer's Practice* is used in hundreds of classrooms across the country each semester.

John works as an analyst and strategist for Willow Research of Chicago, Illinois, and lives in the Charleston, South Carolina, area with his wife, Kathy, and their two dogs, Oscar and Truman.